SCHOLASTIC

D1612244

Reteaching Math
FRACTIONS & DECIMALS

Mini-Lessons, Games & Activities to Review
& Reinforce Essential Math Concepts & Skills

Bob Krech

New York • Toronto • London • Auckland • Sydney
Mexico City • New Delhi • Hong Kong • Buenos Aires

Teaching
Resources

DEDICATION

For Karen, Andrew, and Faith

ACKNOWLEDGMENTS

Thanks to all the teachers and students in the West Windsor-Plainsboro Schools
who helped me learn more about fractions and decimals.
Special thanks to Scott Feder for his math support!

Editor: Maria L. Chang
Cover design by Brian LaRossa
Interior design by Holly Grundon
Interior illustrations by Mike Moran

ISBN-13: 978-0-439-52969-3
ISBN-10: 0-439-52969-7

Table of Contents

Table of Contents (continued)

REPRODUCIBLE STUDENT PAGES

Introduction

Most math books that have the word *reteaching* in the title typically feature many pages of equations and practice problems. The reasoning may be that if students require a concept or skill to be retaught, the best way for them to gain mastery is to practice more of the same. Research does show that some students need more time on a task than others in order to learn a concept. However, if a student does not understand a concept or skill the first time, presenting a series of problems that the student already finds difficult and repeating them, without new knowledge or intervention, will most likely not be successful.

To reteach implies actually teaching again, not merely repeated practice. Students need to have a strong conceptual understanding if they are going to be able to do mathematics with accuracy and comprehension. Without this understanding, math can become meaningless, and students simply work by rote. That's why we've created the Reteaching Math series. You will find this series is different from most reteaching books in that the emphasis is on helping students develop understanding as well as on providing useful practice.

Using a Problem-Solving Approach

The activities, games, and lessons in this book are just plain good instruction, with an emphasis on solving problems and applying math in context. Problem solving is the first process standard listed in the NCTM *Principles and Standards for School Mathematics* (2000). The accompanying statement reads, "Problem solving should be the central focus of all mathematics instruction and an integral part of all mathematical activity." In other words, problem solving is what math is all about. Every lesson here begins with a problem to solve to help create a spirit of inquiry and interest. Practice problems are integrated into the lessons so they are meaningful. Real reteaching!

Providing Context

It is important to provide students with a context to help give learning mathematical skills and concepts meaning. Context helps learners understand how these mathematical ideas and tools are useful and can be applied to real-life problems and situations. Context can be provided by creating a theme that carries throughout all the lessons. In this book, the theme of the Fabulously Fruity Candy Company provides a context in which learning about fractions and decimals is relevant, motivating, and fun. A generous dose of humor is included to help ease the anxiety many students feel over fractions and decimals in

---

Teaching Tip

Math Journal/Notebook

Have students keep their math notes, practice papers, and other work in a math journal/notebook. This can be a simple three-ring binder with some blank lined paper. Throughout this book you will find journal prompts that will help your students solidify their understanding of concepts by writing explanations about the ideas in their own words. As they do this, students will be creating their own personal math reference book. The practice pages, which include a Basics Box, should be kept in the journal as well so students will be able to refer back to previous work to help them with definitions, skills, concepts, and ideas.

particular, and math in general. The use of the overarching candy company theme gives all the lessons a sense of cohesion, purpose, and interest.

Addressing Various Learning Styles

A good way to help all students learn mathematics well is to present ideas through physical, pictorial, and symbolic representations. Research suggests the importance of learning math ideas through modeling with manipulatives. Math concepts need to be experienced on a physical level before pictorial and more abstract representations can be truly understood. Relying completely on symbolic representations (e.g., lots of equations) is rarely enough, particularly in a reteaching situation.

Learning experiences featured here include using manipulatives, drawing pictures, writing equations, reading stories, and playing games to help learners gain a strong conceptual knowledge.

What's Inside?

Activity Lessons – introduce major concepts and skills. Timed to last about 40 minutes, these lessons are designed to help students work on the ideas in a hands-on manner and context to help them understand the meaning behind the math and give them an opportunity to apply it in a fun way.

Practice Pages – are specially designed to provide both practice and a helpful reference sheet for students. Each practice page begins with a **word problem** so students can see how and why the math is useful in solving real problems. Each page also features a **Basics Box**. Here, concepts are carefully presented with words, numbers, pictures, definitions, and step-by-step explanations. **Example problems** help solidify understanding, then a series of problems give students meaningful practice. Finally, a **journal prompt** helps students discuss and explore the concept using pictures, numbers, and words, while providing you with an assessment opportunity that looks at student thinking and understanding. Practice pages can be worked on together in class, assigned to be done independently, or given as homework assignments.

Review Pages – provide students with additional focused practice on a specific math concept. The concept is practiced in a variety of formats and is designed to be completed independently. In addition, a **mixed review** of concepts introduced earlier is included in many review pages. By spiraling the curriculum in this way, students' retention and recall of math ideas is supported. These pages may be used for review, practice, homework, or assessment of students' knowledge and understanding.

How to Use This Book

This book can be used as a replacement unit, as a resource for activities for math workshops or centers, or as a supplement to find engaging ideas to enhance a textbook unit. The lessons and activities are presented in a developmental sequence, but can be used as stand-alone or supplementary learning experiences. Since it's written to accommodate all learners, you can use it to teach fractions and decimals to any class.

About Fractions and Decimals

One important aspect of math is that it can be used as a language to help us communicate efficiently both orally and in writing. Fractions and decimals are like two languages that tell about quantities less than 1, but in different ways. Just as the English word *red* means exactly the same as the Spanish word *rojo*, the fraction 1/4 means exactly the same as the decimal 0.25. Each language has specific instances in which it is most useful. When measuring flour for a cake, fractions come in handy. When converting money amounts from one currency to another, you'll most likely use decimals. The big idea is that fractions and decimals help us communicate about quantities smaller than 1.

Fractions and decimals are discussed in the NCTM Standards under the Number and Operations Standard. The expectations for grades 4–6 focus on:

- developing an understanding of fractions as parts of unit wholes, as parts of a collection, as locations on number lines, and as divisions of whole numbers

- using models, benchmarks, and equivalent forms to judge the size of fractions, decimals, and percents

- developing and using strategies to estimate computations involving fractions and decimals in situations relevant to students' experience

- using visual models, benchmarks, and equivalent forms to add and subtract commonly used fractions and decimals

Within these expectations are more specific objectives. These are addressed in the learning experiences throughout this book and include:

- developing fraction and decimal number sense

- learning and using benchmark fractions (1/16, 1/8, 1/4, 1/2, 3/4) and decimals (0.25, 0.50, 0.75)

- understanding improper fractions and mixed numbers

- changing fractions to decimals

- reducing fractions

- finding equivalent fractions

- ordering and comparing fractions and decimals

- adding and subtracting fractions and decimals

- multiplying and dividing fractions and decimals

Recent international studies on student achievement in mathematics suggest that many students around the world have particular difficulty with fractions and decimals, so it's no surprise that there may be a need at times for reteaching. Using an active, engaging, problem-solving approach, as featured here, can help your students achieve understanding and success.

Part 1: Fractions

Materials

For teacher demonstration only:
- apple
- knife

For each student:
- Practice Page #1 (p. 39)
- Review Page #1 (p. 40)

Teaching Tip

Fractions and Decimals Word Walls

As you begin studying fractions and decimals, display a large piece of chart paper prominently in the room or dedicate part of a bulletin board to serve as a Fractions and Decimals Word Wall. When introducing terms such as *fraction*, *numerator*, and *denominator*, write these words on the wall. Work with the class to create a good definition of each term, including diagrams and examples, and put these on the chart. You may also want students to copy the definition into their math journals or personal math dictionaries. Continue adding to and displaying the word wall throughout the unit.

Can I "Half" an Apple, Please?

(INTRODUCING FRACTIONS)

> **Overview:** When working with fractions, it is important for students to have a good base of understanding. To achieve this understanding, it is helpful to begin with some basic, concrete demonstrations and definitions.

Show an apple to the class and say, "I've got an apple here that I want to share with one of my friends. How can I do that?" (*Many students will likely suggest cutting it into two pieces.*)

Ask students, "How many apples do I have here?" (1) Write the numeral '1' on the board. "Okay, now I'm going to cut it into two equal pieces." Cut the apple in half. "Now, how many apples do I have?" (*Still 1*) "Okay, this is still one apple, but how many pieces are there?" (2)

Hold up one of the two pieces. Ask, "Is this one apple?" (*No, it's just a piece of one apple.*) "How can we talk or write about this piece of apple with numbers? How much of the apple is this?" Explain that there are numbers and words we can use to talk about things that are less than 1. We call these *fractions*. Suggest to students that when they think about the word *fraction*, they might think of the word *fractured*, something that is broken up into pieces.

Say, "Think of fractions as smaller pieces broken from a larger whole, like the pieces of the apple. But keep in mind that there is something special about fraction pieces—fractional pieces are all equal."

Ask students: "Now, how can we write about our piece of apple here? We already said we can't just write '1' because it's less than 1. How many equal pieces did we cut the apple into?" (2) "And this is one of the two pieces. When we write a fraction we write it in two parts. The bottom part of the fraction tells us how many equal parts there are altogether. With our apple, we have two pieces, so we write '2.' This part of the fraction is called the *denominator*. It's the bottom number. To remember denominator, think of 'd' for *downstairs*. That's where the denominator is—downstairs, below the other number."

Continue: "So, our denominator tells us how many pieces there are altogether. The top number tells us how many pieces of the whole we are talking about. In this case, we have one of the two pieces, so we write '1' above the '2.' This two-part number is the fraction $\frac{1}{2}$. It tells us we have 1 of 2 equal pieces." Write the fraction on the board and label the two parts.

$$\frac{1}{2} \quad \begin{array}{l} \text{numerator} \\ \text{denominator} \end{array}$$

Next, cut the apple into fourths and ask the same sorts of questions, while demonstrating how to write:

$$\frac{1}{4} \quad \frac{2}{4} \quad \frac{3}{4}$$

Invite students to do the Clay Fractions activity below if there's time left or use it as a next-day follow-up.

ACTIVITY: **Clay Fractions**

This is a good activity to help you pre-assess students while helping them work towards solidifying their definition of fractions through some hands-on exploration.

Give each student a copy of Practice Page #1, a small ball of clay, a plastic knife, and a sheet of wax paper as a work surface. Review the definitions of *fraction*, *numerator*, and *denominator* in the Basics Box on the Practice Page and try the word problem together. Ask students to cut up their clay into different fractions and then record the different fractions they create with drawings and numbers on their papers. (They can also write the words if they know them.) While students do the clay work, circulate and do individual assessment and instruction to make sure students understand the definition of fraction and can apply this knowledge.

When students are finished, invite them to share one of their clay fractions with the class. While sharing, revisit the definition of fraction by asking, "How do you know this is a fraction?"

ACTIVITY: **Fractions Show-and-Tell**

Help students connect fractions to real-world mathematics and their own experience by encouraging them to look around for examples of fractions. As a homework assignment, ask each student to bring in something that has a fraction written on it. It could be a

Literature Link
....

Apple Fractions
by Jerry Pallotta and Rob Bolster
(Scholastic, 2002)

This picture book uses apples as great visual models for simple fractions and more complex ones. This book works especially well with this introductory lesson.

package, a can of food, a newspaper or magazine advertisement, a tool, a map, or other item. Invite students to share their findings with the class and discuss what the fraction means in relation to the object. Leave these on a display table to use as references and possible objects to help generate word problems.

Materials

For each student:

- Fruit-O Bar Order Forms #1 and #2* (pp. 41–42)
- pencil, colored pencils, or crayons
- Practice Page #2 (p. 43)
- Review Page #2 (p. 44)

*Note: If possible, make double-sided photocopies of Order Forms #1 and #2.

For the teacher:

- Transparencies of Fruit-O Bar Order Forms #1 and #2
- overhead markers

ACTIVITY LESSON #2

The Fabulously Fruity Candy Company Presents Fruit-O Bars

(FRACTIONS OF A WHOLE)

> Overview: Students discover how fractions are a helpful way to discuss quantities that are less than one whole.

Introduce this lesson by discussing different ways people can buy gifts—going to a store or ordering through the mail, the Internet, or the phone. Tell students that they will be processing phone orders for the Fabulously Fruity Candy Company. Say, "We have notes (and/or tapes) of some phone orders and we will be practicing how to record these

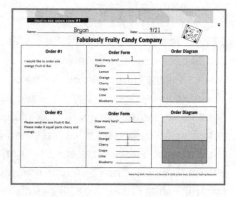

orders on paper. The first candy we will be taking orders for is the Fruit-O Bar. The Fruit-O Bar is about the size of a large Hershey's bar, only it's square and is fruit flavored. Customers can choose the fruit flavor or flavors they want their bar to be."

Pass out copies of the order forms. Display the transparency for each order form on the overhead to use as a model. Tell the class, "When an order is taken, write down how many bars and then indicate what flavor or flavors the bar will be. Let's try one together. In the Order section, you will find notes about the call."

Order #1 – "I would like to order one orange Fruit-O Bar." *(orange = 1)*

Ask students, "How many bars were ordered?" *(1)* "Record it on your order sheet. What flavor?" *(Orange)* "Record that as well. In the last column, there is an order diagram. This helps the candy makers know what they should be making. Color in the Fruit-O Bar diagram with the color for the flavor ordered." *(The entire square should be orange.)* "For quantity, write '1.' Now, let's try a second one."

Order #2 – "Please send me one Fruit-O Bar. Please make it equal parts cherry and orange." *(cherry = 1/2, orange = 1/2)*

Ask, "How many bars were ordered?" *(1)* "Record it on your order sheet. What flavor?" *(Cherry and orange)* "How can we show that?" As students suggest writing 1/2 cherry and 1/2 orange, discuss the fraction and talk about its parts. Tell students, "Remember how we had to talk about amounts that were less than 1 with the apple. Fractions tell about something that is less than 1. In this case, less than 1 whole Fruit-O Bar. Fractions always involve equal parts, so make sure to divide your Fruit-O Bar into 2 equal parts—1 part orange and 1 part cherry."

Order #3 – "I would like to order one Fruit-O Bar. Please make it lime, cherry, lemon, and orange." *(lime = 1/4, cherry = 1/4, lemon = 1/4, orange = 1/4)*

Have students enter the order information and color in the diagram. Call on volunteers to share their answers. Discuss how 1/4 is 1 of 4 equal parts and that the 4 fourths added together make 1 whole. This should be clear on the diagram and order form. Also have students show the different ways the Fruit-O Bar can be divided up into quarters (e.g., horizontal stripes, vertical stripes, four squares, slant lines, and so on).

Order #4 – "I am ordering one Fruit-O Bar for my three sons to share. Bert likes cherry, Bart likes lemon, and Elmo likes grape. Please be sure the bar gives them each a fair share of their favorite flavors." *(cherry = 1/3, lemon = 1/3, grape = 1/3)*

After students have entered the information on their order forms, review their responses together.

This completes the "training session" for the Fabulously Fruity Candy Company order takers.

Teaching Tip

This Call May Be Taped

One very exciting variation you should consider during this series of lessons is to tape-record the customer orders and play them back for students as they read them on their order forms. It is great fun to have different staff members in your school record the orders and have students not only solve the problem but try to identify the mystery callers.

Literature Link

The Hershey's Milk Chocolate Bar Fractions Book
by Jerry Pallotta and Rob Bolster
(Scholastic, 1999)

Great illustrations and easy-to-read text help students see a variety of simple fractions represented by pictures and numbers and Hershey's bars. This is not so much a read-aloud as a book kids will enjoy reading on their own or when you need a pictorial example of specific fractions.

ACTIVITY: **Silly Fraction Stories**

Give each student a piece of writing paper. Ask students to first choose a fraction and draw a diagram of it. Then write a two- or three-sentence silly story about it. For example, someone who drew a square cut into fourths might write: "My mother made us a big mud brownie. I have three dogs. We wanted to share it fairly. We cut it so we would each get a piece." To create an interactive bulletin board, have students write their fraction on the back of the paper or under a flap and challenge others to guess the fraction based on the story and picture. For a more challenging silly story, have students include as many fractions as they can in a five-sentence story. These are great fun to illustrate. Encourage students to put the fractions in their pictures.

Materials

For each student:

- Fruit-O Bar Order Forms #3 and #4* (pp. 45–46)

- pencil, colored pencils, or crayons

- Fraction Strips (p. 47)

- Practice Page #3 (p. 48)

- Review Page #3 (p. 49)

***Note:** If possible, make double-sided photocopies of Order Forms #3 and #4.

ACTIVITY LESSON #3

More Fruit-O Bar Orders

(*EQUIVALENT FRACTIONS*)

> Overview: Students continue to work with fractions of a whole and examine how some of their order form responses are equivalent fractions.

Tell students, "Now that you have been trained as order takers, we have some more complex orders coming in today from the Fabulously Fruity Candy Company. Get your pencil and order forms and get ready to listen." Read or play the tape of the following orders. Use the same review procedures for each order as in Activity Lesson #2.

Order #5 – "I would like one Fruit-O Bar in three equal sections—two should be lemon and one should be lime." *(lemon = 2/3, lime = 1/3)*

Some students may have difficulty dividing the square into thirds. You might suggest using horizontal or vertical stripes.

Order #6 – "I have eight children and want to order one Fruit-O Bar, one section for each child. Seven should be orange and one cherry." *(orange = 7/8, cherry = 1/8)*

Order #7 – "I would like a Fruit-O Bar with four equal pieces—two grape and two cherry." *(grape = 2/4, cherry = 2/4)*

This is a good problem to begin your discussion of equivalent fractions. Ask students, "Is the bar 1/2 grape or 2/4 grape, or do these fractions mean the same thing?" *(They are the same amount, but are written in different ways because they are cut up differently.)*

Draw the following squares on the board:

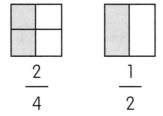

Ask students, "How are these two squares different?" *(One square is divided into 4 equal parts while the other is divided into 2 equal parts.)* "How are they the same?" *(Both squares have the same amount shaded.)* Pointing to the first square, explain to students that because this first square is cut up into 4 equal parts, the denominator for the fraction describing this square would be 4. Ask, "To describe the shaded part of the square, what would the numerator be?" *(2)* Write 2/4 under the first square.

Next, point to the second square and ask students, "If we wanted to describe the part that's shaded in this square, what would the denominator be and why?" *(2, because the square is divided into 2 equal parts)* "What would the numerator be?" *(1)* Write 1/2 under the second square. Ask, "Is 2/4 the same as 1/2?" *(Yes)* Explain to students that 2/4 and 1/2 are called *equivalent fractions* because even though they are different fractions, they name the same amount.

Order #8 – "I need to order a Fruit-O Bar for 16 people so I'll need 16 equal sections. Four should be lemon and the rest blueberry." *(lemon = 4/16, blueberry = 12/16)*

Ask students to find equivalent fractions for 4/16 and 12/16 and put them on their order forms. *(The fraction 4/16 is the same as 1/4, and 12/16 is the same as 3/4.)* Explain to students that even though the bar is cut up into smaller pieces when sixteenths are used, the fraction amounts—4/16 and 1/4, and 12/16 and 3/4—are the same.

As you discuss the idea of equivalent fractions, you might want to share the Fraction Strips on page 47 with students. Challenge students to identify some equivalent fractions using the Fraction Strips.

Teaching Tip

Big Ideas Chart

As you work with students on learning about fractions and decimals, you may want to keep a Big Ideas chart in addition to your word wall. There are certain important ideas about fractions and decimals that students will discover and verbalize. When someone mentions one of these (such as "the smaller the denominator, the bigger the fraction") write it down on the chart and have all students write it in their math journals along with an example using numbers and pictures to show their understanding. This serves as a great personal and classroom reference and reminder.

ACTIVITY: **Equivalent Fractions Game**

To give students more practice in exploring equivalent fractions try this game. Using index cards, make a set of fractions cards (with the fractions 1/2, 1/4, 1/6, 1/8, 1/10, 1/12) and denominator cards (with the numbers 2, 3, 4, 5, 6). Take the fraction cards and put them in one pile. Place the denominator cards in another pile. Players take turns picking a card from the fraction pile and a card from the denominator pile. The player then names an equivalent fraction using the denominator card. If correct, the player keeps both cards. Otherwise, the cards are returned to the bottom of each deck. To make the game even more challenging, have players create their own additional fraction and denominator cards.

Materials

For each student:

- Fruit Drop Order Forms #1 and #2* (pp. 50–51)

- pencil, colored pencils or crayons

- Practice Page #4 (p. 52)

- Review Page #4 (p. 53)

***Note:** If possible, make double-sided photocopies of Order Forms #1 and #2.

ACTIVITY LESSON #4

A New Candy—Fruit Drops!

(FRACTIONS OF A SET)

Overview: **Students explore the idea of fractions of a set.**

Begin today's lesson with a problem or question to get your students thinking in an investigative way. Draw 15 same-size-and-color dots on the board. Write this problem above the picture. "Joe has a bag of candy. He wants to share it fairly with his friends, Tom and Tina. He empties the bag and sees there are 15 candies. How many candies should each person get?" *(5 candies)* Call on students to volunteer answers and discuss. Draw circles around each set of 5 dots to show how the candies would be divided up evenly. Ask students, "What fraction of the bag did each person get?" *(5/15 or 1/3)*

Explain to students that we can use fractions to talk about not only parts of a whole, like a whole apple, but also parts of a set or group of things, like a set of candies or a group of people. Ask them to think of other examples that show a fraction of a set or group of something and discuss.

Tell students, "Today we are going to be helping the Fabulously Fruity Candy Company with some new orders for another one of their famous candies: Fruit Drops. Fruit Drops are small fruity candies that are similar in size and shape to M&M's or Skittles. They come in three different box sizes—small, medium, and large. Small boxes have 4

drops, medium boxes have 8 drops, and large boxes have 16 drops."
Pass out the Order Forms and review together. Listen to the tape or read
the orders below, and work on the first order together as an example.

Order #1 – "I want a small box of Fruit Drops, please. One half should be
blueberry and one half should be orange." *(blueberry = 1/2 or 2 Fruit Drops,
orange = 1/2 or 2 Fruit Drops)*

Students should write the fractions and then color in the diagram. Call
on a volunteer to share his or her answer. Discuss how 1/2 of 4 is 2.

This problem also gives you another opportunity to look at
equivalent fractions. Some students may describe the blueberry as 2/4
and the orange as 2/4. After all, 2 of the 4 pieces are blueberry and 2
of the 4 pieces are orange. From their colored-in diagrams, it should
be clear that 2/4 is equal to 1/2.

Order #2 – "Could I please have a medium box of Fruit Drops with grape,
orange, lime, and cherry?" *(grape = 1/4 or 2 Fruit Drops, orange = 1/4 or
2 Fruit Drops, lime = 1/4 or 2 Fruit Drops, cherry = 1/4 or 2 Fruit Drops)*

If we compare this to the last problem, we see that we are talking
about 2 Fruit Drops for each flavor again. But this time the 2 is 1/4 of
8. How much would 1/4 be of a small box be? *(1 Fruit Drop)* Doing this
problem and discussing its results will help emphasize the idea that
the size of a fractional amount depends on the size of the whole—a
very important concept in fractions.

Order #3 – "One large box of Fruit Drops, please. The flavors I want are lemon,
cherry, blueberry, and grape." *(lemon = 1/4 or 4 Fruit Drops, cherry = 1/4 or
4 Fruit Drops, blueberry = 1/4 or 4 Fruit Drops, grape = 1/4 or 4 Fruit Drops)*

This is an interesting problem for discussion because the previous
caller asked for 4 flavors as well but in a medium box. Now this caller
wants 4 flavors, but in a large box. Contrast the two answers. Students
will see how 1/4 of 8 (2) is larger than 1/4 of 16 (4). Again, we see how
the size of a fraction actually depends on what it is a fraction of.

Order #4 – "Hi! I would like to order a large box of Fruit Drops. Three-fourths
should be cherry, my favorite, and the rest should be lime for my parakeet,
Herbert." *(cherry = 3/4 or 12 Fruit Drops, lime = 1/4 or 4 Fruit Drops)*

When students hear this caller supply the fraction, they often figure
this problem will be easy. But they soon see that they will have to
figure out how much 3/4 of 16 is. Explain to students that drawing a
picture or diagram is often helpful when finding fractions of a set or

Teaching Tip

Avoiding the Mindless Method: Always Ask Why

Many times when young students learn mathematical concepts or skills they memorize a method or procedure and use it by rote, without thinking. Unfortunately, this leads to students who have difficulty solving problems. To help avoid this, make sure students—when learning a new procedure—can explain why they are performing each step. They must be able to tell you the reasoning behind the procedures they use. If they can do this, then you know that they truly have an understanding of the concepts. "Why?" is always a good question for a math journal prompt or as a response to an answer volunteered in class. Ask *why* consistently, however, for both correct and incorrect responses.

Literature Link

Fraction Action by Loreen Leedy (Holiday House, 1994)

A cartoon-style picture book with lots of good situations and examples of fractions in action. These five fun stories tell about characters who use fractions in their everyday lives. Students will enjoy reading this on their own, while teachers will like the situational examples.

group. But they can also use simple multiplication and division. On the board, write:

total number of groups $\longrightarrow$ $\dfrac{3}{4}$ of 16 $\longleftarrow$ total number of items

To find how many is 3/4 of 16, first divide the total number of items (16) by the total number of groups, which is the denominator (4): $16 \div 4 = 4$. Next, multiply this quotient by the particular number of groups we're focusing on, which is the numerator (3): $4 \times 3 = 12$.

$$\dfrac{3}{4} \text{ of } 16 = 12$$

Do a few more examples with students to make sure they understand how the procedure works.

ACTIVITY: **People Fractions Questions and Riddles**

To have students truly "experience" how fractions of sets work, use the students themselves as the objects in the sets. Invite a group of students to come up to the front of the room. Then ask the class to use fractions to describe the group: How many are girls? How many have brown eyes? How many are wearing sneakers? Then have students write down a fraction they notice and challenge their classmates to figure out what feature or characteristic they are focusing on. For example, a student might say, "1/3 of the group is this," and based on the fraction and the people in the group, someone might answer that 1/3 of the group is wearing denim jeans.

Materials

For each student:

• Fruit-O Bar Pieces (p. 54)

• pencil, colored pencils, or crayons

• Practice Page #5 (p. 56)

• Review Page #5 (p. 57)

ACTIVITY LESSON #5

Which Pieces Are the Biggest?

(REDUCING, COMPARING, AND ORDERING FRACTIONS)

Overview: Students will reduce, compare, and order simple fractions.

Announce to students: "The Fabulously Fruity Candy Company is cleaning up some of their candy-making machines, and they have found some perfectly good pieces of Fruit-O Bars left. They have put the pieces in bags and are offering them for sale at very reduced prices. To price them properly and get them organized for display, they have sent along a list of the pieces and flavors. Your job is to put each box of bags in order, from smallest to largest. When we compare fractions to see which is biggest, what do we look at?" Discuss answers.

Box #1 – Orange: 4/8, 3/8, 5/8, 1/8 *(Answer order: 1/8, 3/8, 4/8, 5/8)*

Tell students, "Let's look at the first box of orange pieces. We can see there are bags of 4/8, 3/8, 5/8, and 1/8. These are fairly easy to compare because they all have the same denominator. That means we are talking about same-size pieces. So we know 4/8 would be more than 1/8 because you have 4 of the 8 pieces, not just 1 of the 8 pieces." Draw a diagram to support this idea. Have students try the first box order and discuss answers.

Say, "Now let's look at two fractions that have the same numerator but different denominators and compare them. How about 1/8 and 1/4?" Write these fractions on the board. Ask students, "How do we know which is bigger?" Discuss students' responses, then suggest looking at the denominators. The denominators tell how many pieces the original whole was cut into. Draw two same-size squares. Divide one square into quarters and color in 1/4. Divide the other into eighths and color in 1/8. Say, "When we look at these pictures side by side we can see that the 1/4 is bigger than the 1/8. Why is that?" *(Because quarters are bigger pieces than eighths.)*

Explain, "The key idea to remember is that the bigger the denominator, the smaller the piece. Break up a Fruit-O Bar into fourths and you have 4 pieces. Break it into sixteenths and you have 16 smaller pieces. Imagine hundredths? What a tiny piece 1/100 would be!"

Box #2 – Blueberry: 3/4, 4/4, 1/4, 1/2 *(Answer order: 1/4, 1/2, 3/4, 4/4)*

Tell students, "In this box we have three fractions that have the same denominators—1/4, 3/4, and 4/4. They are easy to put in order, but what about 1/2? We know it's bigger than 1/4 because it has a lower denominator, but how does it compare to the other fractions?" Discuss students' responses.

Explain that one way to make sure that we have a very clear comparison of fractions is to make the fractions have the same denominators. We can convert a fraction to the same denominator as another fraction by multiplying both the numerator and denominator by the same number. So, for 1/2 we can multiply 2 × 2 to make the denominator 4, like the other denominators. We must do the same for the numerator, so 1 × 2 = 2.

$$\frac{1}{2} \times \frac{2}{2} = \frac{2}{4}$$

This gives us a new way of describing this same amount. It would be 2/4, which is the same amount as 1/2. Now we can see where 1/2 would fit in the order.

Box #3 – Cherry: 5/8, 3/8, 1/8, 1/2, 1/4 *(Answer order: 1/8, 1/4, 3/8, 1/2, 5/8)*

Have students try this problem with a partner, then check and discuss together. Guide students to convert 1/4 to 2/8 and 1/2 to 4/8, so all denominators are in eighths.

Box #4 – Lemon: 1/2, 1/8, 3/4, 3/8, 1/4 *(Answer order: 1/8, 1/4, 3/8, 1/2, 3/4)*

Have students work on this problem independently, then compare answers with a partner. Guide students to convert all fractions to eighths for easy comparison. Review students' answers together.

Tell students, "When we put the fractions in order, we had to convert some of them to their equivalent fractions. For example, we had to change 1/2 to 4/8 so we could easily compare it with the other fractions. Sometimes, however, it's easier to work with a fraction when it is in its simplest form. A fraction in its simplest form has the fewest possible pieces. Which of these two fractions—1/2 or 4/8—do you think is in its simplest form?" *(1/2)*

Explain that converting a fraction to its simplest form is also known as *reducing* the fraction. The easiest way to reduce a fraction is to use division. For example, let's take the fraction 8/10. To reduce the fraction down to its simplest form, we divide both the numerator and denominator by the same number. So we look for a number that will divide into both 8 and 10 evenly. In this case, dividing both numbers by 2 will give us 4/5.

$$\frac{8}{10} \div \frac{2}{2} = \frac{4}{5}$$

We can't reduce 4/5 any further because no other number will divide evenly into both 4 and 5, so we know that this fraction is now in its simplest form.

Go over a few more examples with students (such as 6/9, 10/15, and 3/12) to make sure they understand the concept of reducing fractions.

ACTIVITY: **The Squeeze Game – Fraction Version**

Make enough photocopies of the game directions and fraction cards (p. 55) for each pair of students. Consider laminating the cards before cutting them apart so they will be sturdier and last longer. Read aloud the directions and model with a partner how the game is played. Pair up students and give partners a copy of the directions and a set of fraction cards for a fun practice in comparing and ordering fractions.

· ·

ACTIVITY LESSON #6

Multiple Fruit-O Bar Orders

(ADDING AND SUBTRACTING FRACTIONS WITH LIKE DENOMINATORS)

> Overview: Students learn how to add and subtract fractions with like denominators.

Materials

For each student:
- Multiple Fruit-O Bar Order Forms #1 and #2* (pp. 58–59)
- pencil, colored pencils or crayons
- Practice Page #6 (p. 60)
- Review Page #6 (p. 61)

***Note:** If possible, make double-sided photocopies of Order Forms #1 and #2.

Tell the class, "We have some new orders from the Fabulously Fruity Candy Company to fill, but now people are ordering more than one Fruit-O Bar at a time. We will have to use a special new order form." Give each student a copy of the double-sided Multiple Fruit-O Bar Order Form. Say, "When we write these orders down we will need to total the amount of a flavor for the candy makers. So, if someone orders 1/4 orange on their first bar and 1/4 orange on their second bar, how much orange would the candy makers need?" *(2/4 or 1/2 of a bar of orange)*

Draw two Fruit-O Bars on the board and color in 1/4 of one bar orange and 1/4 of the other bar orange. Say, "So if we added these two orange pieces together, we would have 2/4 or 1/2 of an orange bar. We can even write the addition we just did like this:

$$\frac{1}{4} \ + \ \frac{1}{4} \ = \ \frac{2}{4}$$

Adding fractions with the same denominators is very easy because we are adding equal pieces to equal pieces. All we have to do is add the numerators; the denominators stay the same. Let's try some now for the company."

Teaching Tip

Beginning With a Question or Problem

A simple but very powerful teaching strategy is to begin every math lesson with a problem or question that embodies the concept or skill you are teaching in that lesson. This provides a reason and a context for the ideas you want students to learn. Even if you are required to use a textbook lesson, you can still read over the lesson and decide what might be a good opening word problem or question that would require the skill or concept you are going to study. This creates a spirit of inquiry in class and shows that everything you teach has an application and a purpose—to help solve real-life problems.

Order #1 – "I would like to order two Fruit-O Bars, please. One should be 3/4 orange and 1/4 lime. The other should be 3/4 lime and 1/4 orange." *(Totals: orange = 4/4 or 1, lime = 4/4 or 1)*

By adding 3/4 + 1/4 we see that we get 4/4, which is the same as one whole. Write this equation on the board and draw a picture to show how this is correct.

$$\frac{3}{4} \ + \ \frac{1}{4} \ = \ \frac{4}{4} \ = \ 1$$

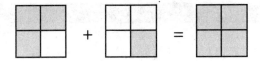

Order #2 – "Please send me two Fruit-O Bars. The first should be 1/4 orange, 1/4 grape, and 2/4 lemon. Make the second bar equal parts lemon, orange, grape, and lime." *(Totals: lemon = 3/4, orange = 2/4, grape = 2/4, lime = 1/4)*

Review students' answers together using both equations and pictures on the board or overhead.

Order #3 – "Could I please have two Fruit-O Bars? The first should be 1/3 each lemon, orange, and blueberry. The second should be 2/3 blueberry and 1/3 orange." *(Totals: lemon = 1/3, orange = 2/3, blueberry = 3/3 or 1)*

Review students' answers together using both equations and pictures on the board or overhead. Emphasize again how we are adding equal-sized parts since the denominators are the same for each piece.

Order #4 – "I'm interested in ordering two Fruit-O Bars. One should be 2/8 cherry and the rest of it lime. The second bar should be 3/8 grape and 3/8 cherry, with the remainder of the bar being lime." *(Totals: cherry = 5/8, grape = 3/8, lime = 8/8 or 1)*

Show students how they can check their answers by adding up the totals of the flavors:

$$\frac{5}{8} \ + \ \frac{3}{8} \ + \ \frac{8}{8} \ = \ \frac{16}{8} \ \text{or 2 bars}$$

ACTIVITY LESSON #7

How Much of That Flavor?

(MIXED NUMBERS AND IMPROPER FRACTIONS)

Overview: Students continue to add and subtract fractions with like denominators with some of the addition leading to sums with mixed numbers.

Materials

For each student:
- Multiple Fruit-O Bar Order Forms #3 and #4* (pp. 62–63)
- pencil, colored pencils or crayons
- Practice Page #7 (p. 64)
- Review Page #7 (p. 65)

*Note: If possible, make double-sided photocopies of Order Forms #3 and #4.

Announce to the class: "We have some new orders for Fruit-O Bars where we will have to add sections of several bars to find a total of each flavor for the candy makers." Read the orders aloud or play the prepared tape of the first order.

Order #1 – "I would like to order two Fruit-O Bars, please. One should be completely orange. The other should be half lime and half orange."
(Totals: orange = 1 1/2, lime = 1/2)

Ask students to look at the number 1 1/2. "What kind of number is it?" *(Mixed number)* Add *mixed number* to your word wall and ask students to define it. *(A mixed number is a number with a whole number part and a fraction part.)*

Show students how the orange sections could also be written and added as:

$$\frac{2}{2} \; + \; \frac{1}{2} \; = \; \frac{3}{2}$$

(You may need to remind students that when the numerator and denominator are the same, that fraction equals 1.) Explain that 3/2 is called an *improper fraction* because the numerator is larger than the denominator. To help students remember this term, you might tell them that it is "improperly built," with the top heavier than the bottom so it might tip over.

Demonstrate how if we were to divide 3 by 2, we would get 1 1/2, a mixed fraction.

$$2\overline{)3} \quad \longrightarrow \quad 1\frac{1}{2}$$

Explain that improper fractions and mixed numbers are two ways to express the same quantity.

Order #2 – "Please send me two Fruit-O Bars. The first should be just lemon. Make the second bar equal parts lemon, orange, grape, and lime." *(Totals: lemon = 1 1/4, orange = 1/4, grape = 1/4, lime = 1/4)*

On the board, write the equation:

$$1 \ + \ \frac{1}{4} \ = \ 1\frac{1}{4}$$

or

$$\frac{4}{4} \ + \ \frac{1}{4} \ = \ \frac{5}{4} \ = \ 1\frac{1}{4}$$

Draw a picture on the board to match this:

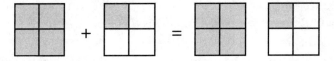

Order #3 – "Could I please have three Fruit-O Bars? The first should be half lemon and half orange. The second should be half lemon and half cherry. And the third one should be equal parts cherry, grape, orange, and lemon." *(Totals: lemon = 1 1/4, orange = 3/4, cherry = 3/4, grape = 1/4)*

Remind students that all the fractions should add up to 3 because there are three whole bars. This is a good review for adding fractions.

Order #4 – "I'm interested in ordering three Fruit-O Bars. One should be 1/4 cherry and the rest of it lime. I want the second and third bar to be identical. Each should be 3/4 grape with the remainder of the bar being lime." *(Totals: cherry = 1/4, grape = 6/4 or 1 1/2, lime = 1 1/4)*

For review, have students demonstrate how to convert the improper fraction 6/4 to a mixed number like 1 1/2.

ACTIVITY: **The Fraction Museum**

Divide the class into five groups and assign each group a day of the week in which to set up a "fraction museum." Using manipulatives (such as interlocking cubes, beans, paper, and counting chips), each student in the group should create his or her own fraction exhibit. Their individual exhibits should be made up of a variety of fraction models, each with a sign that names the fraction in both number and word form (for example, 1/3 and *one third*). All of the group's exhibits together will form that day's Fraction Museum.

While students create their individual exhibits, ask questions that stretch their thinking such as, "Can you show the same fraction two different ways? What is the smallest fraction you can show? Can you show that fraction as part of a group?" The open-ended nature of this activity allows students to really show what they know. They can create as many and as wide a variety of fractions as possible in the time allotted. You might want to require certain minimums though, such as everyone should include models of one half, one fourth, and one eighth. At the end of the period, have each group member explain his or her exhibit to the rest of the class. Ask questions like, "How does that model show 3/4? Which fractions are parts of sets? How else could you make 7/8?" After the tour, that day's exhibits are taken apart and put away so the manipulatives can be used by a new group the following day.

You will find that your class's fraction knowledge builds with each subsequent group's presentation as they listen and learn from one another and try to create new and more original exhibit ideas. The Fraction Museum is a good way to explore and learn about fractions or assess the extent of a student's fraction knowledge. This "museum technique" itself can be used with a variety of math concepts.

ACTIVITY LESSON #8

More Multiple Fruit-O Bar Orders
(ADDING AND SUBTRACTING FRACTIONS WITH UNLIKE DENOMINATORS)

Overview: Students add and subtract fractions with like and unlike denominators.

Tell the class, "More orders for multiple Fruit-O Bars are coming in, but now they are a little more complex. More than one Fruit-O Bar

Materials

For each student:
- Multiple Fruit-O Bar Order Forms #5 and #6* (pp. 66–67)
- pencil, colored pencils, or crayons
- Practice Page #8 (p. 68)
- Review Page #8 (p. 69)

***Note:** If possible, make double-sided photocopies of Order Forms #5 and #6.

is being ordered and the denominators of the fractions are not always the same. Let's see what we can do."

Give each student a copy of the Order Forms. Read the first order or play the prepared tape.

Order #1 – "Could I have two Fruit-O Bars? On the first one, I would like 2 parts orange, 3 parts blueberry, and 3 parts cherry. The second bar should be equal parts lemon, orange, lime, and blueberry." *(Totals: lemon = 1/4, orange = 1/2 or 4/8 or 2/4, lime = 1/4, blueberry = 5/8, cherry = 3/8)*

This problem provides a good opportunity to talk about equivalent fractions again and introduce the concept of adding fractions with unlike denominators. Take the blueberry part as an example. The customer wants 3/8 of the first bar and 1/4 of the second bar to be blueberry. Explain to students that to add the two fractions, we must first change the denominators to *like denominators*. An easy way to do that is to change the lower denominator to match the higher one. In this case, change 1/4 to eighths. To do this, multiply both the numerator and denominator by 2 to get 2/8. Now we can add 3/8 and 2/8 to get 5/8.

$$\frac{3}{8} + \frac{1}{4} = \frac{}{}$$

$$\frac{1}{4} \times \frac{2}{2} = \frac{2}{8}$$

$$\frac{3}{8} + \frac{2}{8} = \frac{5}{8}$$

Coloring in the diagrams really helps students see how the addition works.

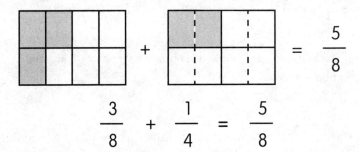

$$\frac{3}{8} + \frac{1}{4} = \frac{5}{8}$$

You may even want students to cut out the pieces and rearrange them together so they can see the addition take place physically.

Order #2 – "I would like two Fruit-O Bars. The first bar is for my family. Please make it with 2 parts lemon, 2 parts orange, 2 parts cherry, and 2 parts grape. The second bar is for some of my friends. I would like it to have 4 parts lemon, 4 parts orange, 4 parts cherry, and 4 parts grape." *(Totals: lemon = 1/2, orange = 1/2, cherry = 1/2, grape = 1/2)*

This is a good problem for looking at the relationship between fourths, eighths, sixteenths, and halves—the most common fractions students will deal with in their day-to-day lives.

Order #3 – "I need three Fruit-O Bars. One should be 1/2 lemon with the rest equal parts lime and blueberry. The second bar should be 2 parts lemon, 1 part blueberry, and 1 part lime. The third bar should be 1/2 lemon with the rest equal parts orange, cherry, grape, and blueberry." *(Totals: lemon = 3/2 or 1 1/2, orange = 1/8, cherry = 1/8, grape = 1/8, lime = 1/2, blueberry = 5/8)*

This provides another good practice for adding fractions with different denominators and for dealing with mixed numbers and improper fractions. Invite students to share their answers with the class.

Order #4 – Make this order a free choice for students. Invite them to order three different bars for themselves. Encourage them to get at least three different flavors in each bar to make it interesting.

ACTIVITY: **Your Name in Fractions**

Students can create interesting riddles using fractions and their names. For example, say a student's name is James. For people to guess his name, he would give them fractional clues about the letters in his name, like this: "My name is the first 1/4 of *jump*, the second 2/3 of *tam*, the first 1/3 of *egg*, and the last 1/2 of *is*." To create the riddles, have students write the clues on one side of a piece of construction paper and illustrate them. On the other side of the paper, have them spell out their names. For extra challenge, have them do both first and last names. This makes for a fun and interactive bulletin board as viewers try to guess the names.

Materials

For each student:

- Pieces of Fruit-O Bars (p. 70)
- pencil
- Practice Page #9A (p. 71)
- Review Page #9A (p. 72)
- Practice Page #9B (p. 73)
- Review Page #9B (p. 74)

ACTIVITY LESSON #9

Pieces of Fruit-O Bars

(MULTIPLYING AND DIVIDING FRACTIONS)

> **Overview:** Students will learn about multiplying and dividing simple fractions by whole numbers and by fractions.

Tell the class, "The Fabulously Fruity Candy Company has lots of leftover pieces of Fruit-O Bars. They plan on combining these pieces to make full-size Fruit-O Bars. I have a copy of the data sheet they use to keep track of the leftover pieces that they want to combine." Pass out a copy of the Pieces of Fruit-O Bars activity page to each student.

Say, "Let's look at the pieces of cherry that are left over. Count them up. How many are there?" *(5 pieces; each piece is 3/4 of a bar)* "We could add these to get a total. That would be:

$$\frac{3}{4} + \frac{3}{4} + \frac{3}{4} + \frac{3}{4} + \frac{3}{4} = \frac{15}{4}$$

This is repeated addition, right? What's another way to do repeated addition?" *(Multiplication)*

Explain to students that the above addition expression is the same $5 \times 3/4$. Write this on the board. To multiply a whole number by a fraction, first convert the whole number to a fraction form. In this case, we can write 5 as 5/1. *(5 ÷ 1 = 5)* We set up the expression so it reads:

$$\frac{5}{1} \times \frac{3}{4}$$

We multiply across the numerators and get $5 \times 3 = 15$. Then we multiply across the denominators and get $1 \times 4 = 4$. This gives us an answer of 15/4—the same answer as when we added.

$$\frac{5}{1} \times \frac{3}{4} = \frac{15}{4}$$

We can convert this improper fraction to a mixed number by dividing 15 by 4 to get 3 3/4, which is an easier number to understand.

Tell students, "Multiplying fractions like this is easy. Just multiply the numerators and then the denominators. If you are working with a whole number, convert it to a fraction first by making that number the numerator and 1 its denominator. Now let's try the rest of this order with a partner." Have students work with a partner to complete the order form. Review all answers together and discuss.

Tell students, "Let's say you have 6/8 of a lemon Fruit-O Bar and you want to find out how many 1/4 pieces you can make out of it. How can you find out how many 1/4 pieces make 6/8?" (*Divide the 6/8 bar by 1/4*) Write the following on the board:

$$\frac{6}{8} \div \frac{1}{4} = \ ?$$

The first step is to invert or flip the divisor. So in this case, 1/4 becomes 4/1. Then multiply the numerators and denominators:

$$\frac{6}{8} \times \frac{4}{1} = \frac{24}{8} = 3$$

Reduce the answer to its simplest form, and we get 3. It takes three 1/4 pieces to make 6/8. Draw a diagram on the board to show this.

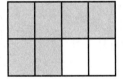

Give a few more examples and work through them with students until they understand both concepts of multiplying and dividing fractions. Distribute copies of the various practice and review pages for independent practice and/or homework.

Part 2: Decimals

Materials

For each student:
- Super-Sour Square Order Form #1 (p. 76)
- pencil, colored pencils, or crayons
- Practice Page #10 (p. 79)
- Review Page #10 (p. 80)
-

For the teacher:
- Transparency of The Super-Sour Square (p. 75)
- overhead markers

ACTIVITY LESSON #10

Super-Sour Squares

(INTRODUCING DECIMALS)

> **Overview:** Students will learn about decimals and their relationship to fractions as a way to communicate about quantities less than one whole. Decimal quantities are explored to hundredths.

Tell the class, "The Fabulously Fruity Candy Company has a new candy called Super-Sour Squares, and they want you to help take orders for them. They come in the same fruit flavors as Fruit-O Bars, but they are sour flavors and larger square bars." Display the transparency of the Super-Sour Square page on the overhead.

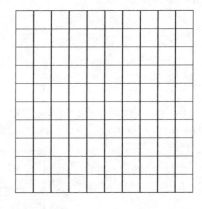

Say, "As you can see, this candy can be scored in a variety of ways. *Scored* means to be cut partway through, as we see in some chocolate bars, so it's easy to break off pieces. A Super-Sour Square can be cut into 100 small pieces. It can also be cut into Super-Sour Strips with 10 strips making up a square." Show this by outlining each strip of 10 squares on your overhead Super-Sour Square.

Ask students, "When a Super-Sour Square is cut into 10 strips, how can we talk about one of those strips? It wouldn't be one Super-Sour Square. How much of a Super-Sour Square is it?" *(1/10)* "Right, it is 1/10 of the whole thing. We can also talk about it with decimals."

Explain to students that decimals are another way to communicate about quantities less than one whole. For example, we see decimals when we talk about money. We can write one dollar as $1.00. Write "$1.00" on the board. For half of a dollar, we can write it as $0.50. Write "$0.50" on the board as well. Pointing to both dollar amounts on the board, tell students that these are examples of a *decimal*. The point or period is called a *decimal point*. It separates the whole number from the fractional part.

Ask students, "If we had 1/10 of a dollar, how would we write that?" (*$0.10 or ten cents or one dime*) Explain that writing $0.10 is a way to write the amount with a decimal. Decimals are a good way to write quantities that are less than one whole, especially when you have to add, subtract, multiply, or divide them. That's because they fit easily into equation formats and there is no need for converting or reducing as with fractions.

Focus students' attention toward the place value chart at the bottom of the Super-Sour Square page. With an overhead marker, write "1" under the ones space. Say, "This is how we would write 1 Super-Sour Square." Erase the 1 and write "1" under the tens space and "0" under the ones space. Say, "Here's how we would write 10 Super-Sour Squares." Erase the numbers again and write "1" under the hundreds space, "0" under the tens space, and "0" under the ones space. Ask students, "What is this number?" (*100*)

Explain that to write numbers less than 1, we use a decimal point. This point separates the numbers that tell us about numbers that are 1 or larger from numbers that are less than 1. Anything to the right of the decimal point talks about pieces or fractions.

Say, "The first space to the right of the decimal point is the tenths place. We can write about the Super-Sour Strips here. Remember, there are 10 Super-Sour Strips in one Super-Sour Square." Color in one strip of the Super-Sour Square. Ask students, "How would we write about this strip as a fraction?" (*1/10*) Tell students that there is another way to write about this strip using decimals. On the place value chart, write 0 under the ones place and 1 under the tenths place. Explain to students that the decimal 0.1 is called *one tenth*, pointing to the word *tenth* on the chart.

Ask, "What if we were talking about 3 of the 10 strips? What fraction would that be?" (*3/10*) "What is the decimal equivalent?" (*0.3*) "How would we write that in words?" (*Three tenths*) On the board, write:

$$\frac{3}{10} = 0.3 = \text{three tenths}$$

Teaching Tip
....

Shopping with Money and Decimals

Students have seen amounts of money written in decimal form. This is a good real-world connection to emphasize. Have students do some shopping by bringing in food store circulars or newspaper advertisements as well as any grocery receipts from home. Ask them to tell about how decimals are used in these examples. For a fun activity, give students a dollar amount and ask them to "go shopping" using the circulars to create a receipt from the store reflecting their imaginary purchases.

Literature Link
....

America's Champion Swimmer: Gertrude Ederle by David Adler (Harcourt, 2000)

This nonfiction picture book tells the story of Gertrude Ederle, the first woman to swim the English Channel. Decimals are commonly used to record measurements of distance and time. As students learn about Gertrude's perseverance they will also find out about the numerical aspects of her records.

Do the same sequence with 5/10 and 0.5. Then ask students, "What is 5/10 in simplest form?" (*1/2*) Guide students to understand that the decimal 0.5 is equivalent to the fraction 1/2. Color in 5 strips on the Super-Sour Square, if necessary.

Next, move to the hundredths place on the place value chart. Remind students that there are 100 small squares in one Super-Sour Square. Color in one of the small squares. Ask, "If we were talking about 1 small square in a Super-Sour Square, what fraction would that be?" (*1/100*) "What do you think is its decimal equivalent?" (*0.01*) Write this on the place value chart. Guide students to notice that the numeral 1 is now under the hundredths place. Explain to students that 0.01 is called *one hundredth*, pointing to the word *hundredth* on the chart.

Tell students, "Say we were talking about 12 small squares. How would we write that as a fraction?" (*12/100*) "How would we write that as a decimal?" (*0.12*) Write the decimal number on the place value chart. Tell students that this number is called *twelve hundredths*, because the last digit is in the hundredths place.

Then color in half of the Super-Sour Square and guide students to notice that 50/100 is the same as 5/10, so 0.50 = 0.5. So fifty hundredths is equal to five tenths. Do as many examples as you feel are helpful.

Tell students, "Now let's see if we can fill in an order for Super-Sour Squares using fractions and decimals." Distribute copies of the Super-Sour Square Order Form to students. Have them fill the following four orders. You can read them aloud or play them on a tape recorder. Students should write a fraction and decimal for each and color in the diagram to match.

Order #1 – "I would like one Super-Sour Square, please. Please make 1/10 of it orange and the rest lime." (*orange = 1/10 = 0.1, lime = 9/10 = 0.9*)

Have students fill in their Super-Sour Square Order Form. They should write the flavor (*orange*), the fraction (*1/10*), and the decimal (*0.1*). Ask, "How much of the rest of the bar would be lime?" (*9/10 and 0.9*)

Order #2 – "Could I have a Super-Sour Square that's 1/2 lemon and 1/2 cherry? Thank you." (*lemon = 1/2 = 0.5, cherry = 1/2 = 0.5*)

Encourage students to write any equivalent fractions and decimals they may see, such as 1/2 or 5/10 or 50/100 as well as 0.5 and 0.50. These all fit the diagram.

Order #3 – "Could I have a Super-Sour Square, please? I would like 6/10 lemon and the rest blueberry. Thank you very much!" *(lemon = 6/10 = 0.6, blueberry = 4/10 = 0.4)*

Order #4 – "Please make me one Super-Sour Square. How about 3/10 cherry, 3/10 lemon, and the rest orange? Thank you." *(cherry = 3/10 = 0.3, lemon = 3/10 = 0.3, orange = 4/10 = 0.4)*

ACTIVITY: Decimals Show-and-Tell

Ask students to bring in items from home that have decimals printed on them. Food packages are great for this. Have students copy the decimal on a piece of paper, then write the decimal in word form and write a corresponding fraction. Students will find that many packages already have the fraction on them. Give each student an opportunity to show his or her item and tell about the decimal on it.

ACTIVITY: Fraction/Decimal Matching Game

Make enough photocopies of the game directions (p. 77) and fraction and decimal cards (p. 78) for each pair of students. To play, students must match up fractions and their equivalent decimals to create pairs. The player with the most pairs wins.

. . . .

ACTIVITY LESSON #11

More Super-Sour Squares

(COMPARING AND ORDERING DECIMALS TO HUNDREDTHS)

> Overview: Students continue working with decimals into hundredths and begin comparing and ordering them.

Tell the class, "We've got more orders from the Fabulously Fruity Candy Company." Pass out a double-sided copy of the blank Super-Sour Square Order Form to each student. Read aloud or play a tape of the orders, telling students to write them on the order form. Review and discuss each order response on the board or overhead. Make sure students use pictures, fractions, and decimals in each order.

Materials

. . . .

For each student:

- Super-Sour Square Order Form #2* (p. 81)

- pencil, colored pencils or crayons

- Practice Page #11 (p. 83)

- Review Page #11 (p. 84)

*Note: If possible, make double-sided photocopies of this blank Order Form for each student.

Literature Link

···

NBA Math Skills: Slam and Jam: Charts, Graphs and Statistics, Geometry and Measurement, Fractions, Decimals and Percents (Scholastic, 1997)

This is a great book to begin delving into sports records, most of which are recorded in fractions, decimals, and percents. In addition to interesting sports facts and statistics, this book offers lots of challenging problems using this real-life data.

Order #1 – "Hi. Could I have a Super-Sour Square that's 0.8 orange and the rest blueberry? Thanks!" *(orange = 0.8 = 8/10, blueberry = 0.2 = 2/10)*

Remind students to write both the fractions and decimals on the order form.

When reviewing this order ask students, "Which is more—the 0.8 orange or the 0.2 blueberry?" Write the two numbers one above the other on the board, making sure the decimals line up. Tell students, "When you compare numbers that have decimals, it is important to line up the decimal points so we can see clearly what digit is in each place. Begin in the largest place—in this case, the ones place—and compare the digits place value by place value, going from left to right."

$$0.8$$

$$0.2$$

Show how the ones place is the same for each number—0. But when we look at the tenths place (to the right of the decimal point), we see orange has 8 and blueberry has only 2. Discuss why 0.8 is larger and how it actually means 8 out of 10 pieces, while 0.2 is only 2 out of 10 pieces.

Order #2 – "Please make me a Super-Sour Square that has 25 pieces of lime and 75 pieces of orange." *(lime = 0.25 = 1/4 = 25/100, orange = 0.75 = 3/4 = 75/100)*

This is the first example asking students to use hundredths. Ask students, "Which is more—the 0.25 lime or the 0.75 orange?" *(0.75)* Write the two numbers again on the board with the decimal points lined up. Remind students that when comparing decimals, they should always begin by lining up the decimals and then look at the largest place value. With these two numbers, the ones place is again the largest and both have 0 in the ones place. Looking at the tenths place, we see that there are 7 tenths of orange and only 2 tenths of lime. So without having to look at the hundredths place, we already know that the orange is more.

Now ask students, "Which is more—0.8 or 0.75?" *(0.8)* Again, remind the class to line up the decimal points and begin at the highest place value. Both numbers have 0 in the ones place. Moving on, we see that one number has 8 in the tenths place and the other has 7 in the tenths place. Right away we know that the 8 tenths is more even though the 7 tenths is followed by 5 hundredths. Explain to students that we could extend the 0.8 and write it as 0.80 if that would help make the comparison clearer because 0.8 (eight tenths) is equal to 0.80 (eighty hundredths).

Order #3 – "Hello. Please send me a Super-Sour Square that's 1/2 lemon, 0.2 grape, and 3/10 cherry." *(lemon = 1/2 = 0.5 = 5/10 = 50/100, grape = 0.2 = 2/10 = 20/100, cherry = 3/10 = 0.3 = 30/100)*

This problem provides a mix of fractions and decimals, but remains in tenths. When you review student work on this order, have them compare the three decimals again.

Order #4 – "Hi. I would like one Super-Sour Square that's got 50 pieces of lemon, 25 pieces of cherry, and 25 pieces of lime. Thank you very much." *(lemon = 50/100 = 0.5 = 0.50, cherry = 25/100 = 0.25, lime = 25/100 = 0.25)*

This problem focuses on hundredths. Have students compare the three decimals again for review.

Order #5 – "Good afternoon. Could I have a Super-Sour Square that has 1 piece of cherry. I don't really like cherry, but my sister does. I want to have 50 pieces of orange. I love orange. The rest could be blueberry for my parents. Thanks a lot." *(cherry = 1/100 = 0.01, orange = 50/100 = 0.5 = 0.50, blueberry = 49/100 = 0.49)*

This is a good example to begin a discussion on adding and subtracting decimals. Also, make a point of discussing the difference between 0.10 and 0.01. Have students write these three decimals in order and discuss the comparison.

Order #6 – "Hello. I'm interested in ordering a Super-Sour Square that is 3/10 lemon. It should also have 60 pieces of grape and 0.1 could be orange." *(lemon = 3/10 = 30/100 = 0.3, grape = 60/100 = 0.60 = 0.6, orange = 1/10 = 10/100 = 0.10)*

Have students write these three decimals in order and discuss the comparison.

Once Orders #1 through #6 are completed and reviewed, ask students to call out all of the decimal numbers used in the orders. Write these on the board in the order given or put them on index cards that can be moved around easily. Ask students to copy the numbers on a separate sheet of paper and put them in order from

Teaching Tip
....

Labeling

Often, students don't label a fraction or decimal answer ("3/4 of the apple or 0.75 of the apple" vs. just "3/4 or 0.75"). They leave the number standing alone, unrelated to anything else. You may want to insist that students label fraction and decimal answers, so instead of just writing "1/4," they would write "1/4 of the apple." This reinforces the idea that the fraction stands for something—that it has a meaning and is not just a symbol floating around.

smallest to largest. Call on volunteers to come to the board and rewrite or rearrange the numbers into the proper order. Remind students to line up the decimal points and to begin in the largest place value, working their way to the smallest as they compare. *(The order from smallest to largest is: 0.01, 0.1, 0.2, 0.2, 0.25, 0.25, 0.25, 0.3, 0.3, 0.49, 0.5, 0.5, 0.5, 0.6, 0.75, 0.8)*

Order #7 – Create an order for students. Use whatever numbers you would like students to have further practice with.

Order #8 – Ask students to create their own order for fun.

ACTIVITY: **The Squeeze Game – Decimal Version**

Make enough photocopies of the game directions and decimal cards (p. 82) for each pair of students. Consider laminating the cards before cutting them apart so they will be sturdier and last longer. Read aloud the directions and model with a partner how the game is played. Pair up students and give partners a copy of the directions and a set of decimal cards for a fun practice in comparing and ordering decimals.

- -

Materials

For each student:
- 3 copies of Multiple Super-Sour Square Order Form (p. 85)
- pencil, colored pencils or crayons
- Practice Page #12 (p. 86)
- Review Page #12 (p. 87)

For the teacher:
- Transparency of Multiple Super-Sour Square Order Form
- overhead markers

ACTIVITY LESSON #12

Ordering More Than One Super-Sour Square

(ADDING AND SUBTRACTING DECIMALS)

> Overview: Students add and subtract decimals with resulting whole and mixed numbers.

Distribute copies of the Multiple Super-Sour Square Order Form to students. Tell them, "Callers are now ordering more than one Super-Sour Square, and we need to record these new orders using fractions and decimals to ensure accuracy. We also need to calculate the total amount of a flavor for the candy makers. For example, if an order asks for one square that is 1/4 lemon and another square that is 1/2 lemon, we need to let the candy makers know the total amount of lemon they'll need."

Display the Multiple Super-Sour Square Order Form transparency on the overhead. Ask students, "So if the customer wants one square to be 1/4 lemon, how much of the first Super-Sour Square should we color in?" *(1/4 or 25 small squares)* Color in a quarter of the first Super-Sour Square. Ask, "What is the decimal equivalent?" *(0.25)* Continue: "The customer wants the second square to be 1/2 lemon, so how much of the second Super-Sour Square should we color in?" *(1/2 or 50 small squares)* Color in half of the second Super-Sour Square. Ask, "What is the decimal equivalent?" *(0.5 or 0.50)* On the board, write:

$$
\begin{array}{r}
0.25 \\
+\ 0.50 \\
\hline
\end{array}
$$

Explain to students that when adding (or subtracting) decimals, the most important thing to remember is that the decimal points should always be lined up, including the decimal point for the sum. Then they can add the digits the same way that they would with whole numbers—from right to left, regrouping as needed. So in this case, the answer would be 0.75.

$$
\begin{array}{r}
0.25 \\
+\ 0.50 \\
\hline
0.75
\end{array}
$$

If we wanted to know how much more lemon the second square has than the first, we would subtract 0.25 from 0.50, like this:

$$
\begin{array}{r}
0.50 \\
-\ 0.25 \\
\hline
0.25
\end{array}
$$

Emphasize that the process of adding and subtracting decimals is the same as with whole numbers and that the key is to keep the decimal in its proper position.

Read or play your prepared tape of Order #1. After playing or reading each order, have students share and discuss their answers.

Teaching Tip

Providing a Context

All students need a reason to learn mathematical concepts and skills. Students who need extra help in math in particular need a good reason why they're doing what they're doing. Why do we have fractions and decimals? A good way to address this question is to put kids in a problem-solving situation, like the Fabulously Fruity Candy Company problems, where they see the need for fractions. You might also look for articles in newspapers and magazines that include fractions and decimals. Use these (or have students use these) to create fraction and decimal word problems that are answered by the data in the article. This helps students think creatively and mathematically while building that real-world connection to how fractions and decimals are used in everyday life.

Remind students that they need to calculate the total amount of a flavor for each order. Review these on the board with equations and pictures. Have students check their addition by subtracting.

Order #1 – "I would like to order two Super-Sour Squares. For the first one, I would like 1/2 cherry and the rest equal parts orange and lemon. The second should be 0.50 lemon and 0.25 orange and the rest cherry." *(Totals: lemon = 75/100 = 0.75, orange = 50/100 = 0.50, cherry = 75/100 = 0.75)*

Order #2 – "I would like to order three Super-Sour Squares, please. For the first bar I would like to have 7/10 orange and the rest grape. The second bar should be 0.20 cherry, 30/100 lemon, and the rest grape. The third bar should be all cherry." *(Totals: lemon = 30/100 = 0.30, orange = 70/100 = 0.70, cherry = 120/100 = 1.20, grape = 80/100 = 0.80)*

Order #3 – "I want to order some Super-Sour Squares. I want mine to be mostly blueberry, I think about 6/10, and the rest can be lime. The second bar should have 80 pieces of blueberry with the rest orange. I want the third bar to be 1/2 grape and 1/10 orange." *(Totals: orange = 30/100 = 0.30, lime = 40/100 = 0.40, grape = 50/100 = 0.50, blueberry = 140/100 = 1.40, total for all bars = 260/100 = 2.60)*

Note that in this order, the third bar is not a complete bar so the total order is only 2 6/10 or 2 3/5 bars.

. . . .

Materials

. . . .

For each student:

• pencil

• Pieces of Super-Sour Squares (p. 88)

• colored pencils or crayons

• Practice Page #13 (p. 89)

• Review Page #13 (p. 90)

ACTIVITY LESSON #13

Pieces of Super-Sour Squares
(*Multiplying Decimals*)

Overview: Students learn how multiplying decimals is similar in procedure to multiplying whole numbers, but that the decimal placement is all important for a correct answer.

Tell the class, "I've just been informed that the Fabulously Fruity Candy Company has lots of leftover pieces of Super-Sour Squares.

They want to combine these pieces to make full Super-Sour Squares so they've grouped the smaller pieces by flavor. I have a list of leftover pieces that you will need to work through. Let's look at an example."

Draw four 1/2-size Super-Sour Square pieces on the board or overhead. Say, "Here's a group of 4 orange Super-Sour Square pieces. You can see that each piece is 1/2 of a full-size square. We could write that as 1/2. How would we write it as a decimal?" *(0.5)* "So we have 4 halves or 4 × 1/2 or 4 × 0.5. How much would that be altogether?" *(2 full-size Super-Sour Squares)*

Explain that one way to solve this problem or to check that it works is to multiply the 4 by 0.5. Set this up as a regular multiplication problem, making sure that the place value of each number is lined up properly and the decimal point is brought down into the answer space in its proper position. Remind students that since 4 is a whole number, the digit is technically to the left of a decimal point. Add a decimal point and a 0 to the right of the number to emphasize that 4 is the same as 4.0. Demonstrate this on the board:

$$
\begin{array}{r}
^{2} \\
4.0 \\
\times\ 0.5 \\
\hline
2.00
\end{array}
$$

Explain to students that when multiplying decimals, the key thing to remember is to count the places to the right of the decimal point in both factors. This will also be the number of places to the right of the decimal point in the product. In this example, there are two places to the right of the decimal point. So the product also has two places to the right of its decimal point. Point out to students, however, that 2.00 is the same as 2.

Have students work with a partner to complete the Pieces of Super-Sour Squares activity page. Review finished order forms and discuss.

Materials

For each student:

- Super-Sour Squares Special Order Form (p. 91)
- pencil , colored pencils, or crayons
- Practice Page #14 (p. 92)
- Review Page #14 (p. 93)

Teaching Tip

Calculator and Diagram Use

For problems involving decimals and fractions with operations, it is often helpful to have students check their work using a calculator and/or a diagram. Have students try the manual computation first. If they find that a calculator check results in a different answer, they should go back and redo the computation but accompany their work with a diagram, preferably on graph paper. This helps students work toward developing number sense and encourages them to seek meaningful answers, not just go through a mechanical process.

ACTIVITY LESSON #14

Sharing Super-Sour Squares
(DIVIDING DECIMALS)

Overview: Students learn how the process of dividing decimals is just like division with whole numbers except for keeping track of the decimal.

Tell the class, "We have some special requests from the Fabulously Fruity Candy Company. Some people have ordered unusual amounts of Super-Sour Squares and now they want the amounts divided up evenly among them." Give each student a copy of the Special Order Form and say, "Here are the orders I'm talking about. You can see the first one at the top."

Draw a picture of one complete Super-Sour Square and half of another on the board. Ask students, "If we were to share this 1 1/2 Super-Sour Square equally among 3 people, what would you estimate each person would get? Half, or less than half?" This will help students begin to think about what a sensible answer would be. Discuss students' responses.

Ask, "So if we are sharing this amount of candy, what operation would we use to do the sharing?" *(Division)* "So we divide the amount that we have by the number of people. We would divide 1.5 by 3."

Set up the problem on the board and demonstrate how to divide, emphasizing that the decimal point for the quotient should be placed directly above the dividend's decimal point:

$$3)\overline{1.5} \quad .5$$
$$\underline{15}$$
$$0$$

Conclude, "When we divide the 1.5 by 3 we see that the answer is 0.5 or 1/2, which makes sense because then each of the 3 people would get 1/2 Super-Sour Square. We can check that because 0.5 + 0.5 + 0.5 = 1.5 or 1 1/2."

Have students work with a partner to complete the order form, then invite students to share their answers and discuss them together.

Name: _____ Date: _____

Harry cut a peach into 8 pieces. Each piece was equal. He kept 1 piece and gave the rest to his friends. How much of the peach did he keep?

BASICS BOX

Fraction – A number that describes a part of a whole or a part of a group. For example, $\frac{1}{4}$ of the marbles are black.

Denominator – The number below the line in a fraction. It tells how many equal parts are in the whole. For example, $\frac{1}{2}$ of the circle is shaded.

 $\dfrac{1}{2}$ ⟶ denominator

Numerator – The number above the line in a fraction. It tells how many of the equal parts are being focused on. For example, $\frac{2}{6}$ of the rectangle is shaded.

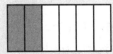 $\dfrac{2}{6}$ ⟶ numerator

Harry kept 1 of 8 pieces of the peach, or $\frac{1}{8}$ of the peach.

Your Clay Fractions

Use a ball of clay and a plastic knife to create different fractions.
Record your fractions below.

Picture	Picture
Number _____	Number _____
Word _____	Word _____

JOURNAL

Write a sentence with a fraction in it. Draw a picture that matches the sentence and shows the fraction.

Name: _____   Date: _____

Introducing Fractions

1. 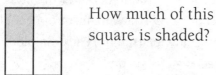 How much of this
   circle is shaded?

   _____

2. How much of this
   square is shaded?

   _____

3. 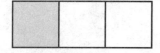 How much of this
   rectangle is shaded?

   _____

4. $\dfrac{1}{8}$ What is the
   denominator? _____

   What is the
   numerator? _____

5. 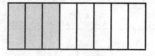 Is this square
   divided into fourths?

   _____

   Why or why not?

   _____

Match the picture and the fraction.

6.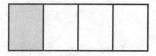

$\dfrac{5}{16}$

7.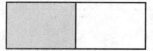

$\dfrac{1}{2}$

8.

$\dfrac{1}{4}$

9.

$\dfrac{3}{8}$

10.

$\dfrac{1}{3}$

Name: _____   Date: _____

Fabulously Fruity Candy Company

Order #1

I would like to order one orange Fruit-O Bar.

Order Form

How many bars? _____

Flavors:

    Lemon _____

    Orange _____

    Cherry _____

    Grape _____

    Lime _____

    Blueberry _____

Order Diagram

Order #2

Please send me one Fruit-O Bar.
Please make it equal parts cherry and orange.

Order Form

How many bars? _____

Flavors:

    Lemon _____

    Orange _____

    Cherry _____

    Grape _____

    Lime _____

    Blueberry _____

Order Diagram

Name: _____

Date: _____

Fabulously Fruity Candy Company

Order #3

I would like to order one Fruit-O Bar. Please make it lime, cherry, lemon, and orange.

Order Form

How many bars? _____

Flavors:

Lemon _____

Orange _____

Cherry _____

Grape _____

Lime _____

Blueberry _____

Order Diagram

Order #4

I am ordering one Fruit-O Bar for my three sons to share. Bert likes cherry, Bart likes lemon, and Elmo likes grape. Please be sure the bar gives them each a fair share of their favorite flavors.

Order Form

How many bars? _____

Flavors:

Lemon _____

Orange _____

Cherry _____

Grape _____

Lime _____

Blueberry _____

Order Diagram

Reteaching Math: Fractions and Decimals © 2008 by Bob Krech, Scholastic Teaching Resources

Name: _____   Date: _____

WORD PROBLEM

John saw this pizza in the cafeteria. He wanted plain pizza. How much of the pizza could John have?

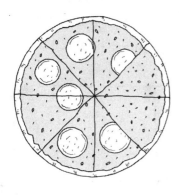

BASICS BOX

Fractions tell about parts of wholes. It is a way to talk about amounts less than 1. Some common fractions are:

$\frac{1}{2}$ (one half) $\frac{1}{3}$ (one third)

$\frac{1}{4}$ (one fourth or one quarter) $\frac{1}{8}$ (one eighth)

The bottom number of a fraction is the *denominator*. It tells us how many equal pieces the whole has been divided into. The top number is the *numerator*. It tells us how many of the equal pieces we are focusing on.

We see that John's pizza has 8 equal pieces—6 pieces have toppings and 2 are plain. So John could have $\frac{2}{8}$ of the pizza.

PRACTICE

Write the fraction to match the shaded part of the picture.

1. _____

2. _____

3. _____

4. _____

5.  _____

6. _____

7. _____

8. _____

Draw a fraction. Write the number.

9. _____

10. _____

JOURNAL

Charlene's birthday cake was $\frac{1}{8}$ blue, $\frac{3}{8}$ red, $\frac{1}{8}$ orange, and $\frac{3}{8}$ yellow icing. Draw a picture of Charlene's cake and color it in.

Name: _____ Date: _____

Fractions of a Whole

Draw a picture to match each fraction.

1. $\frac{1}{4}$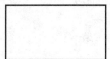

2. $\frac{1}{3}$

3. $\frac{2}{3}$

4. $\frac{1}{2}$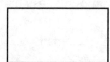

5. $\frac{3}{4}$

6. $\frac{1}{8}$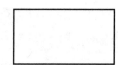

7. Color in this Fruit-O Bar so $\frac{1}{4}$ is lemon, $\frac{1}{4}$ is grape, $\frac{1}{4}$ is cherry and $\frac{1}{4}$ is blueberry.

Write the fraction for each picture.

8.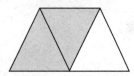

_____

9.

_____

10.

_____

Review:

11. What is the numerator in $\frac{7}{8}$? _____

12. What is the denominator in $\frac{1}{10}$? _____

13. If $\frac{1}{3}$ of a Fruit-O Bar is cherry and the rest is orange, how much is orange? _____

Reteaching Math: Fractions and Decimals © 2008 by Bob Krech, Scholastic Teaching Resources

Name: _____   Date: _____

Fabulously Fruity Candy Company

Order #5

I would like one Fruit-O Bar in three equal sections—two should be lemon and one should be lime.

Order Form

How many bars? _____

Flavors:

Lemon _____

Orange _____

Cherry _____

Grape _____

Lime _____

Blueberry _____

Order Diagram

Order #6

I have eight children and want to order one Fruit-O Bar, one section for each child. Seven should be orange and one cherry.

Order Form

How many bars? _____

Flavors:

Lemon _____

Orange _____

Cherry _____

Grape _____

Lime _____

Blueberry _____

Order Diagram

Name: _____

Date: _____

Fabulously Fruity Candy Company

Order #7

I would like a Fruit-O Bar with four
equal pieces—two grape and two cherry.

Order Form

How many bars? _____

Flavors:

Lemon _____

Orange _____

Cherry _____

Grape _____

Lime _____

Blueberry _____

Order Diagram

Order #8

I need to order a Fruit-O Bar for 16
people so I'll need 16 equal sections.
Four should be lemon and the rest
blueberry.

Order Form

How many bars? _____

Flavors:

Lemon _____

Orange _____

Cherry _____

Grape _____

Lime _____

Blueberry _____

Order Diagram

Reteaching Math: Fractions and Decimals © 2008 by Bob Krech, Scholastic Teaching Resources

Name: _____ Date: _____

Fraction Strips

1											

| $\frac{1}{2}$ | | | | | | $\frac{1}{2}$ | | | | | |

| $\frac{1}{3}$ | | | | $\frac{1}{3}$ | | | | $\frac{1}{3}$ | | | |

| $\frac{1}{4}$ | | | $\frac{1}{4}$ | | | $\frac{1}{4}$ | | | $\frac{1}{4}$ | | |

| $\frac{1}{5}$ | | $\frac{1}{5}$ | | $\frac{1}{5}$ | | $\frac{1}{5}$ | | $\frac{1}{5}$ | | | |

| $\frac{1}{6}$ | | $\frac{1}{6}$ | | $\frac{1}{6}$ | | $\frac{1}{6}$ | | $\frac{1}{6}$ | | $\frac{1}{6}$ | |

| $\frac{1}{8}$ | $\frac{1}{8}$ | $\frac{1}{8}$ | $\frac{1}{8}$ | $\frac{1}{8}$ | $\frac{1}{8}$ | $\frac{1}{8}$ | $\frac{1}{8}$ | | | | |

| $\frac{1}{10}$ | $\frac{1}{10}$ | $\frac{1}{10}$ | $\frac{1}{10}$ | $\frac{1}{10}$ | $\frac{1}{10}$ | $\frac{1}{10}$ | $\frac{1}{10}$ | $\frac{1}{10}$ | $\frac{1}{10}$ | | |

| $\frac{1}{12}$ | $\frac{1}{12}$ | $\frac{1}{12}$ | $\frac{1}{12}$ | $\frac{1}{12}$ | $\frac{1}{12}$ | $\frac{1}{12}$ | $\frac{1}{12}$ | $\frac{1}{12}$ | $\frac{1}{12}$ | $\frac{1}{12}$ | $\frac{1}{12}$ |

Name: _____ Date: _____

Flip finished $\frac{2}{4}$ of his homework. Flop finished $\frac{1}{2}$ of her homework. "Got more done than you," said Flip to Flop. Is he right?

BASICS BOX

Can two fractions, like $\frac{2}{4}$ and $\frac{1}{2}$, name the same amount? Let's look at a picture.

$$\frac{2}{4} \qquad \frac{1}{2}$$

So what's different? Well, even though $\frac{2}{4}$ of a square is the same as $\frac{1}{2}$ of the same-size square, it is cut into more, smaller pieces. The denominator in $\frac{2}{4}$ tells us that there are 4 pieces. The denominator in $\frac{1}{2}$ tells us there are only 2 pieces, but the pieces are bigger.

PRACTICE

Using the fraction strips on page 47, find some equivalent fractions for those listed below. List as many as you can.

1. $\frac{1}{2}$ =

2. $\frac{1}{4}$ =

3. $\frac{1}{3}$ =

4. $\frac{2}{5}$ =

5. $\frac{2}{3}$ =

6. $\frac{1}{6}$ =

7. $\frac{3}{4}$ =

JOURNAL

Are $\frac{2}{3}$ and $\frac{8}{12}$ equivalent fractions? Tell how you know. Use words, numbers, and pictures.

Reteaching Math: Fractions and Decimals © 2008 by Bob Krech, Scholastic Teaching Resources

Name: _____   Date: _____

Equivalent Fractions

Circle the pairs that are equivalent fractions.

1. $\frac{1}{4}$ $\frac{1}{8}$

2. $\frac{2}{4}$ $\frac{2}{8}$

3. $\frac{1}{4}$ $\frac{2}{8}$

4. $\frac{1}{2}$ $\frac{2}{4}$

5. $\frac{3}{8}$ $\frac{6}{12}$

6. $\frac{6}{16}$ $\frac{3}{8}$

7. $\frac{2}{10}$ $\frac{1}{5}$

8. $\frac{7}{8}$ $\frac{3}{4}$

Fill in the blanks to create equivalent fractions.

9. $\frac{3}{4} = \frac{6}{\quad}$

10. $\frac{1}{3} = \frac{\quad}{6}$

11. $\frac{9}{10} = \frac{\quad}{20}$

12. $\frac{1}{2} = \frac{\quad}{16}$

13. $\frac{\quad}{8} = \frac{1}{4}$

14. $\frac{2}{\quad} = \frac{1}{8}$

15. $\frac{7}{\quad} = \frac{14}{16}$

16. $\frac{2}{\quad} = \frac{6}{9}$

17. Write four equivalent fractions for $\frac{1}{2}$.

   a.

   b.

   c.

   d.

Review: Write a fraction for each picture.

18. 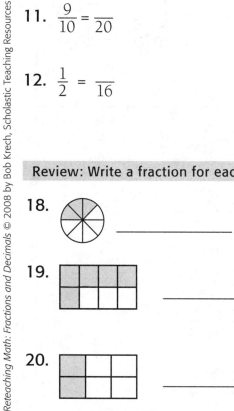 _____

19. _____

20. _____

21. What is the numerator in $\frac{3}{9}$? _____

22. What is the denominator in $\frac{5}{8}$? _____

50

Name: _____   Date: _____

Fabulously Fruity Candy Company

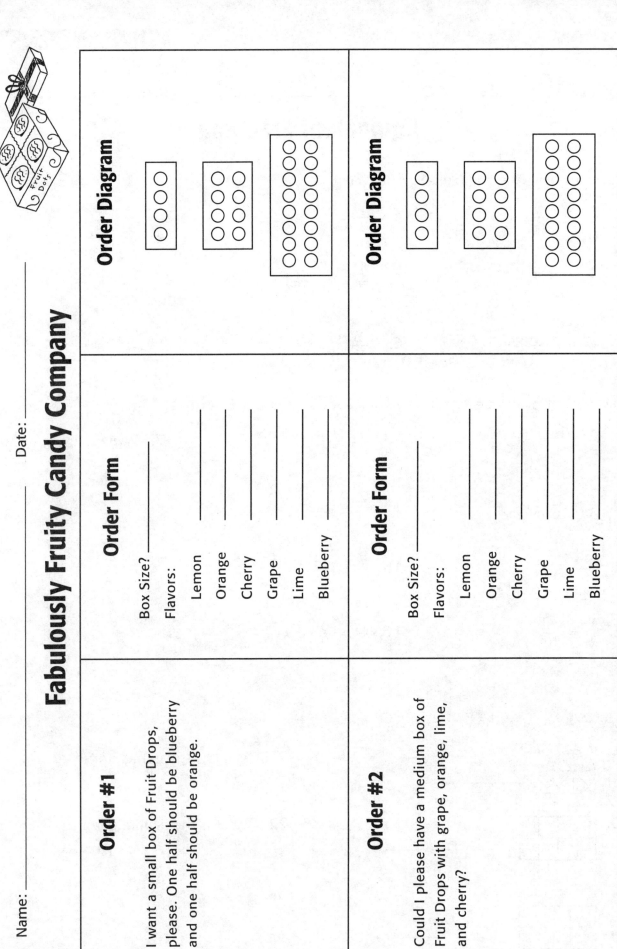

Order #1

I want a small box of Fruit Drops, please. One half should be blueberry and one half should be orange.

Order Form

Box Size? _____

Flavors:

Lemon _____

Orange _____

Cherry _____

Grape _____

Lime _____

Blueberry _____

Order Diagram

Order #2

Could I please have a medium box of Fruit Drops with grape, orange, lime, and cherry?

Order Form

Box Size? _____

Flavors:

Lemon _____

Orange _____

Cherry _____

Grape _____

Lime _____

Blueberry _____

Order Diagram

Reteaching Math: Fractions and Decimals © 2008 by Bob Krech, Scholastic Teaching Resources

Name: _____ Date: _____

Fabulously Fruity Candy Company

Order #3

One large box of Fruit Drops, please. The flavors I want are lemon, cherry, blueberry, and grape.

Order #4

Hi! I would like to order a large box of Fruit Drops. Three fourths should be cherry, my favorite, and the rest should be lime for my parakeet, Herbert.

Order Form

Box Size? _____

Flavors:

Lemon _____
Orange _____
Cherry _____
Grape _____
Lime _____
Blueberry _____

Order Form

Box Size? _____

Flavors:

Lemon _____
Orange _____
Cherry _____
Grape _____
Lime _____
Blueberry _____

Order Diagram

Order Diagram

Name: _____ Date: _____

WORD PROBLEM

There were 21 students in Mr. Smart's math class. $\frac{1}{3}$ voted for dogs as their favorite animal. The rest of the class voted for cats. How many votes did dogs get?

BASICS BOX

Pictures or diagrams, along with multiplication and division, can help you find fractions of a set or group.

 21 students

To find $\frac{1}{3}$ of 21:

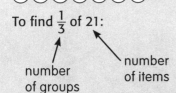

number of groups   number of items

Divide the total number of items (21) by the number of groups (3).

21 ÷ 3 = 7 students voted for dogs

number in a group

What if $\frac{2}{3}$ voted for dogs? How many students would that be? We already know 21 ÷ 3 = 7 students in a group. To know about 2 of the 3 groups, we multiply:

2 x 7 = 14 number of students in 2 groups

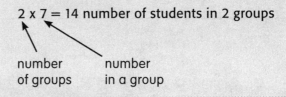

number of groups   number in a group

EXAMPLE

There were 24 cats in the yard. $\frac{1}{4}$ were striped. How many striped cats?

$\frac{1}{4}$ of 24

24 ÷ 4 = _____

PRACTICE

1. $\frac{3}{8}$ of 16 = _____

2. $\frac{1}{5}$ of 25 = _____

3. $\frac{1}{2}$ of 24 = _____

4. $\frac{5}{6}$ of 18 = _____

5. $\frac{2}{9}$ of 18 = _____

6. $\frac{1}{10}$ of 100 = _____

JOURNAL

Explain with words, numbers, and pictures how you would find $\frac{5}{6}$ of 30.

Reteaching Math: Fractions and Decimals © 2008 by Bob Krech, Scholastic Teaching Resources

Name: _____   Date: _____

Fractions of a Set

Write the fraction for each shaded part of the set.

1. _____ ●○○○

2. _____ ●●○○

3. _____ ●○

4. _____ △△△△△△

5. _____ △△△△△

6. _____ ▢▢▢▢▢▢▢▢

Match the fraction with the picture.

7. ●●●●○

8. ▢▢▢▢▢▢▢▢

9. △△△△△

10. ●●○○

$\dfrac{1}{2}$

$\dfrac{4}{5}$

$\dfrac{3}{9}$

$\dfrac{1}{5}$

11. How much is $\dfrac{1}{2}$ of 16? _____

12. How much is $\dfrac{1}{3}$ of 12? _____

13. 4 is what fraction of 16? _____

Review: Make these fractions equivalent.

14. $\dfrac{1}{4} = \dfrac{}{8}$

15. $\dfrac{}{3} = \dfrac{2}{6}$

16. $\dfrac{5}{8} = \dfrac{10}{}$

Review: What fraction of the shape is shaded?

17.   _____

18.   _____

Name: _____   Date: _____

Fruit-O Bar Pieces

Directions: Put each bag of pieces in order from smallest to largest.

Box #1: Orange

$\frac{4}{8}$ $\frac{3}{8}$ $\frac{5}{8}$ $\frac{1}{8}$

Order: _____ , _____, _____, _____

Box #2: Blueberry

$\frac{3}{4}$ $\frac{4}{4}$ $\frac{1}{4}$ $\frac{1}{2}$

Order: _____ , _____, _____, _____

Box #3: Cherry

$\frac{5}{8}$ $\frac{3}{8}$ $\frac{1}{8}$ $\frac{1}{2}$ $\frac{1}{4}$

Order: _____ , _____, _____, _____, _____

Box #4: Lemon

$\frac{1}{2}$ $\frac{1}{8}$ $\frac{3}{4}$ $\frac{3}{8}$ $\frac{1}{4}$

Order: _____ , _____, _____, _____, _____

Reteaching Math: Fractions and Decimals © 2008 by Bob Krech, Scholastic Teaching Resources

Name: _____   Date: _____

The Squeeze Game – Fraction Version

Materials: Fraction cards (below)   Players: 2

1. Place the 0 card at one end of a desk and the 1 card at the other end. Place the 1/2 card right in the middle of the 0 and 1 cards.

2. Shuffle the fraction cards. Deal six cards to each player.

3. Players take turns placing a card so it touches either side of another card on the desk. Cards must be placed in increasing order. A card may not be placed between two other touching cards.

4. The object of the game is to place as many cards as you can. A round is over when a player can no longer place any of his or her cards. The number of cards left in a player's hand is his or her score.

5. At the end of a round, return any leftover cards to the deck and shuffle. Repeat steps 1 to 4 to play another round.

6. After six rounds, add up players' points. The player with the least number of points wins.

Cut out the cards below.

0	1	$\dfrac{1}{2}$	$\dfrac{1}{3}$
$\dfrac{2}{3}$	$\dfrac{1}{4}$	$\dfrac{3}{4}$	$\dfrac{1}{5}$
$\dfrac{2}{5}$	$\dfrac{3}{5}$	$\dfrac{4}{5}$	$\dfrac{1}{6}$
$\dfrac{5}{6}$	$\dfrac{1}{8}$	$\dfrac{3}{8}$	$\dfrac{5}{8}$
$\dfrac{7}{8}$	$\dfrac{1}{10}$	$\dfrac{7}{10}$	$\dfrac{9}{10}$

Name: _____   Date: _____

Elena cut up her steak into 16 bite-size pieces. She ate 8 of these.
What fraction of her steak did she eat? Reduce the answer to simplest form.

BASICS BOX

A fraction in simplest form has the fewest possible pieces. If you look at the equivalent fractions $\frac{3}{4}$ and $\frac{6}{8}$, $\frac{3}{4}$ is in simplest form because it has only 4 pieces instead of 8.

In the above problem, Elena ate $\frac{8}{16}$ of her steak. An easy way to reduce this fraction to its simplest form is to use division. First, divide both the numerator and denominator by the same number. We need to find a number that will divide into 8 and 16 evenly.

$$\frac{8}{16} \div \frac{2}{2} = \frac{4}{8}$$

If we divide by 2, we get $\frac{4}{8}$. But this fraction can be reduced even further. If we divide 8 and 16 by 4, we get $\frac{2}{4}$, which is still not the simplest form. We need to find the **greatest common factor** between the numerator and denominator. The greatest common factor between 8 and 16 is 8. When we divide both the numerator and denominator by that number, we get $\frac{1}{2}$, which cannot be reduced further.

$$\frac{8}{16} \div \frac{8}{8} = \frac{1}{2}$$

PRACTICE

Reduce these fractions to simplest form. Look for the greatest common factor to divide with. Circle the fractions that are already in simplest form.

1. $\frac{2}{10} =$ 6. $\frac{2}{8} =$

2. $\frac{7}{14} =$ 7. $\frac{9}{12} =$

3. $\frac{9}{21} =$ 8. $\frac{6}{8} =$

4. $\frac{12}{15} =$ 9. $\frac{7}{10} =$

5. $\frac{19}{20} =$ 10. $\frac{9}{15} =$

Circle the larger fraction.
Reduce to simplest form to help.

11. $\frac{5}{12}$ or $\frac{1}{3}$ 13. $\frac{2}{9}$ or $\frac{2}{16}$

                                           14. $\frac{3}{5}$ or $\frac{8}{10}$

12. $\frac{1}{4}$ or $\frac{2}{16}$

Put these fractions in order.
Reduce to simplest form to help.

15. $\frac{1}{2}$ $\frac{3}{18}$ $\frac{6}{9}$

16. $\frac{3}{5}$ $\frac{2}{10}$ $\frac{16}{20}$

JOURNAL

Tell how you would reduce $\frac{8}{12}$ to its simplest form. Use pictures, words, and numbers.

Reteaching Math: Fractions and Decimals © 2008 by Bob Krech, Scholastic Teaching Resources

Name: _____   Date: _____

Reducing, Comparing, and Ordering Fractions

Reduce these fractions to simplest form.

1. $\frac{6}{8} =$

2. $\frac{5}{10} =$

3. $\frac{3}{6} =$

4. $\frac{12}{16} =$

5. $\frac{10}{12} =$

6. $\frac{3}{15} =$

7. $\frac{5}{20} =$

8. $\frac{2}{8} =$

Circle the larger fraction.

9. $\frac{1}{16}$ $\frac{1}{18}$

10. $\frac{3}{4}$ $\frac{7}{8}$

11. $\frac{1}{4}$ $\frac{2}{3}$

12. $\frac{5}{16}$ $\frac{3}{8}$

13. $\frac{1}{2}$ $\frac{14}{16}$

14. $\frac{4}{12}$ $\frac{1}{4}$

Put these fractions in order from smallest to largest.

15. $\frac{1}{2}$ $\frac{3}{16}$ $\frac{7}{16}$ $\frac{1}{4}$

16. $\frac{3}{10}$ $\frac{3}{5}$ $\frac{3}{8}$ $\frac{3}{4}$

17. $\frac{1}{2}$ $\frac{3}{4}$ $\frac{1}{8}$ $\frac{2}{3}$

Name: _____   Date: _____

Fabulously Fruity Candy Company

Order #1

I would like to order two Fruit-O Bars, please. One should be $\frac{3}{4}$ orange and $\frac{1}{4}$ lime. The other should be $\frac{3}{4}$ lime and $\frac{1}{4}$ orange.

Flavor	Bar 1	Bar 2	Bar 3	Totals
Lemon				
Orange				
Cherry				
Grape				
Lime				
Blueberry				

Order Diagram

Order #2

Please send me two Fruit-O Bars. The first should be $\frac{1}{4}$ orange, $\frac{1}{4}$ grape, and $\frac{2}{4}$ lemon. Make the second bar equal parts lemon, orange, grape, and lime.

Flavor	Bar 1	Bar 2	Bar 3	Totals
Lemon				
Orange				
Cherry				
Grape				
Lime				
Blueberry				

Order Diagram

58

Reteaching Math: Fractions and Decimals © 2008 by Bob Krech, Scholastic Teaching Resources

Name: _____   Date: _____

Fabulously Fruity Candy Company

Order #3

Could I please have two Fruit-O Bars?
The first should be $\frac{1}{3}$ each lemon,
orange, and blueberry. The second
should be $\frac{2}{3}$ blueberry and $\frac{1}{3}$ orange.

Order Diagram

Flavor	Bar 1	Bar 2	Bar 3	Totals
Lemon				
Orange				
Cherry				
Grape				
Lime				
Blueberry				

Order #4

I'm interested in ordering two Fruit-O
Bars. One should be $\frac{2}{8}$ cherry and the
rest of it lime. The second bar should
be $\frac{3}{8}$ grape and $\frac{3}{8}$ cherry, with the
remainder of the bar being lime.

Order Diagram

Flavor	Bar 1	Bar 2	Bar 3	Totals
Lemon				
Orange				
Cherry				
Grape				
Lime				
Blueberry				

Name: _____   Date: _____

WORD PROBLEM

Zelda washed $\frac{1}{8}$ of the family car. Zena washed $\frac{3}{8}$ of the car.
How much of the car got washed?

BASICS BOX

To add fractions with like denominators:

1. Add the numerators.

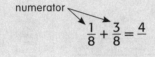

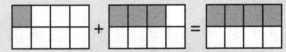

2. The denominators stay the same.

$$\frac{1}{8} + \frac{3}{8} = \frac{4}{8}$$

Like denominators mean same-size pieces

denominator

3. Simplify, if possible.

$$\frac{4}{8} = \frac{1}{2}$$

4. Label your answer: $\frac{1}{2}$ of the car

To subtract fractions with like denominators, do the same:

1. Subtract the numerators.

numerator

$$\frac{4}{8} - \frac{3}{8} = \frac{1}{}$$

2. The denominators stay the same.

$$\frac{4}{8} - \frac{3}{8} = \frac{1}{8}$$ denominator

3. Simplify, if possible. ($\frac{1}{8}$ is in simplest form)

PRACTICE

Solve these problems. Remember to simplify.

1. $\frac{5}{8} + \frac{1}{8} =$

2. $\frac{1}{4} + \frac{2}{4} =$

3. $\frac{2}{7} + \frac{4}{7} =$

4. $\frac{3}{8} - \frac{3}{8} =$

5. $\frac{5}{16} - \frac{4}{16} =$

6. $\frac{4}{6} - \frac{1}{6} =$

7. $\frac{1}{3} + \frac{2}{3} =$

8. $\frac{5}{10} - \frac{3}{10} =$

9. $\frac{2}{9} + \frac{1}{9} =$

10. $\frac{7}{16} - \frac{4}{16} =$

JOURNAL

Solve this equation. Draw a picture to prove your answer. $\frac{1}{6} + \frac{3}{6} = ?$

Reteaching Math: Fractions and Decimals © 2008 by Bob Krech, Scholastic Teaching Resources

Name: _____   Date: _____

Adding and Subtracting Fractions with Like Denominators

Add. Remember to simplify.

1. $\frac{3}{8} + \frac{3}{8} =$

2. $\frac{2}{6} + \frac{3}{6} =$

3. $\frac{3}{8} + \frac{1}{8} =$

4. $\frac{3}{4} + \frac{1}{4} =$

5. $\frac{4}{16} + \frac{3}{16} =$

6. $\frac{1}{5} + \frac{3}{5} =$

Subtract. Remember to simplify.

7. $\frac{3}{5} - \frac{2}{5} =$

8. $\frac{3}{4} - \frac{2}{4} =$

9. $\frac{5}{8} - \frac{3}{8} =$

10. $\frac{10}{16} - \frac{5}{16} =$

11. $\frac{8}{9} - \frac{6}{9} =$

12. $\frac{2}{3} - \frac{1}{3} =$

Add or subtract. Remember to simplify.

13. $\frac{3}{10} + \frac{5}{10} =$

14. $\frac{8}{16} - \frac{4}{16} =$

15. $\frac{2}{4} + \frac{2}{4} =$

16. $\frac{3}{8} + \frac{4}{8} =$

17. $\frac{4}{6} - \frac{4}{6} =$

18. $\frac{6}{7} - \frac{2}{7} =$

Name: _____

Date: _____

Fabulously Fruity Candy Company

Order #1

I would like to order two Fruit-O Bars, please. One should be completely orange. The other should be half lime and half orange.

Flavor	Bar 1	Bar 2	Bar 3	Totals
Lemon				
Orange				
Cherry				
Grape				
Lime				
Blueberry				

Order Diagram

Order #2

Please send me two Fruit-O Bars. The first should be just lemon. Make the second bar equal parts lemon, orange, grape, and lime.

Flavor	Bar 1	Bar 2	Bar 3	Totals
Lemon				
Orange				
Cherry				
Grape				
Lime				
Blueberry				

Order Diagram

Reteaching Math: Fractions and Decimals © 2008 by Bob Krech, Scholastic Teaching Resources

Name: _____ Date: _____

Fabulously Fruity Candy Company

Order #3

Could I please have three Fruit-O Bars? The first should be half lemon and half orange. The second should be half lemon and half cherry. And the third one should be equal parts cherry, orange, and lemon.

Flavor	Bar 1	Bar 2	Bar 3	Totals
Lemon				
Orange				
Cherry				
Grape				
Lime				
Blueberry				

Order Diagram

Order #4

I'm interested in ordering three Fruit-O Bars. One should be $\frac{1}{4}$ cherry and the rest of it lime. I want the second and third bar to be identical. Each should be $\frac{3}{4}$ grape with the remainder of the bar being lime.

Flavor	Bar 1	Bar 2	Bar 3	Totals
Lemon				
Orange				
Cherry				
Grape				
Lime				
Blueberry				

Order Diagram

Name: _____ Date: _____

Joe had $\frac{3}{4}$ of a pizza. Joanne gave him $\frac{3}{4}$ of another pizza. How much pizza does Joe have?

BASICS BOX

When we add the fractions, the result is as follows:

$$\frac{3}{4} + \frac{3}{4} = \frac{6}{4}$$

$\frac{6}{4}$ is called an *improper fraction* because the numerator is larger than the denominator. We can convert an improper fraction to a *mixed number*. A mixed number is a number that includes a whole number and a fraction—a clearer way to see how much we actually have. To convert an improper fraction to a mixed number, simply divide the numerator by the denominator:

$$\frac{6}{4}$$

$$\begin{array}{r} 1 \\ 4\overline{)6} \\ \underline{4} \\ 2 \end{array}$$

$1\frac{2}{4}$ or $1\frac{1}{2}$

So we can see that Joe got $1\frac{1}{2}$ pizzas.

To convert a mixed number into an improper fraction: $1\frac{3}{4} = \frac{7}{4}$

1. Multiply the denominator by the whole number.
2. Add the sum to the numerator.
3. Keep the same denominator as the original fraction.

Write each improper fraction as a whole or mixed number.

1. $\frac{5}{3}$ =

2. $\frac{10}{5}$ =

3. $\frac{7}{2}$ =

4. $\frac{9}{4}$ =

5. $\frac{8}{8}$ =

Write each mixed number as an improper fraction.

6. $2\frac{2}{3}$ =

7. $1\frac{1}{2}$ =

8. $3\frac{1}{2}$ =

9. $1\frac{3}{4}$ =

10. $2\frac{1}{8}$ =

Complete using <, >, or =.

11. $\frac{13}{16}$ ◯ $2\frac{1}{6}$

12. $1\frac{2}{9}$ ◯ $\frac{12}{9}$

13. $\frac{7}{10}$ ◯ $1\frac{3}{10}$

JOURNAL

Using words, pictures, and numbers, tell how you would change $\frac{9}{6}$ to a mixed number. How would you change $1\frac{4}{5}$ to an improper fraction?

Reteaching Math: Fractions and Decimals © 2008 by Bob Krech, Scholastic Teaching Resources

Name: _____ Date: _____

Mixed Numbers and Improper Fractions

Write each improper fraction as a whole or mixed number.

1. $\dfrac{16}{8} =$

2. $\dfrac{16}{16} =$

3. $\dfrac{16}{4} =$

4. $\dfrac{5}{2} =$

5. $\dfrac{10}{7} =$

6. $\dfrac{4}{3} =$

Write each mixed number as an improper fraction.

7. $1\dfrac{1}{4} =$

8. $2\dfrac{1}{5} =$

9. $1\dfrac{3}{5} =$

10. $2\dfrac{4}{7} =$

11. $3\dfrac{1}{3} =$

12. $1\dfrac{7}{10} =$

Add or subtract. Remember to simplify.

13. $\dfrac{1}{3} + \dfrac{1}{3} =$

14. $\dfrac{3}{5} + \dfrac{1}{5} =$

15. $\dfrac{7}{8} - \dfrac{4}{8} =$

16. How much is $\dfrac{1}{4}$ of 16? _____

17. Put these fractions in order from smallest to largest: $\dfrac{3}{16}$ $\dfrac{1}{8}$ $\dfrac{3}{4}$ $\dfrac{1}{2}$

Name: _____

Date: _____

Fabulously Fruity Candy Company

Order #1

Could I have two Fruit-O Bars? On the first one, I would like 2 parts orange, 3 parts blueberry, and 3 parts cherry. The second bar should be equal parts lemon, orange, lime, and blueberry.

Flavor	Bar 1	Bar 2	Bar 3	Totals
Lemon				
Orange				
Cherry				
Grape				
Lime				
Blueberry				

Order Diagram

Order #2

I would like two Fruit-O Bars. The first bar is for my family. Please make it with 2 parts lemon, 2 parts orange, 2 parts cherry, and 2 parts grape. The second bar is for some of my friends. I would like it to have 4 parts lemon, 4 parts orange, 4 parts cherry, and 4 parts grape.

Flavor	Bar 1	Bar 2	Bar 3	Totals
Lemon				
Orange				
Cherry				
Grape				
Lime				
Blueberry				

Order Diagram

Reteaching Math: Fractions and Decimals © 2008 by Bob Krech, Scholastic Teaching Resources

Name: _____   Date: _____

Fabulously Fruity Candy Company

Order #3

I need three Fruit-O Bars. One should be $\frac{1}{2}$ lemon with the rest equal parts lime and blueberry. The second bar should be 2 parts lemon, 1 part blueberry, and 1 part lime. The third bar should be $\frac{1}{2}$ lemon with the rest equal parts orange, cherry, grape, and blueberry.

Flavor	Bar 1	Bar 2	Bar 3	Totals
Lemon				
Orange				
Cherry				
Grape				
Lime				
Blueberry				

Order Diagram

Order #4

Flavor	Bar 1	Bar 2	Bar 3	Totals
Lemon				
Orange				
Cherry				
Grape				
Lime				
Blueberry				

Order Diagram

Name: _____   Date: _____

Jake had $\frac{1}{4}$ of the candy bar. Jinx had $\frac{1}{8}$. How much of the candy bar did they have altogether?

Pete had $\frac{7}{8}$ of an apple. He ate $\frac{3}{4}$ of the apple. How much apple was left?

BASICS BOX

To help Jake and Jinx, we have to add fractions with unlike denominators:

$$\frac{1}{4} + \frac{1}{8} =$$

First, we must change the unlike denominators to like denominators. The best way is to find an equivalent fraction. Try to change the lower denominator to match the higher. So, $\frac{1}{4}$ needs to be changed to eighths. Multiply the numerator and denominator by the same number; in this case, 2.

$$\frac{1}{4} \times \frac{2}{2} = \frac{2}{8}$$

Now, we can add $\frac{2}{8}$ and $\frac{1}{8}$.

$$\frac{2}{8} + \frac{1}{8} = \frac{3}{8}$$

Jake and Jinx ate $\frac{3}{8}$ of the candy bar altogether.

To subtract fractions with different denominators, first find an equivalent fraction to make like denominators:

$$\frac{7}{8} - \frac{3}{4} =$$

$$\frac{3}{4} \times \frac{2}{2} = \frac{6}{8}$$

Then subtract the numerators to find the answer.

$$\frac{7}{8} - \frac{6}{8} = \frac{1}{8} \text{ of Pete's apple was left}$$

JOURNAL

Write a word problem where you must add or subtract fractions to get the answer. Solve and show your method.

PRACTICE

Add these fractions.

1. $\frac{1}{2} + \frac{1}{8} =$

2. $\frac{3}{10} + \frac{3}{5} =$

3. $\frac{2}{3} + \frac{1}{6} =$

4. $\frac{1}{4} + \frac{5}{8} =$

Subtract these fractions.

5. $\frac{5}{12} - \frac{1}{6} =$

6. $\frac{1}{3} - \frac{1}{9} =$

7. $\frac{4}{5} - \frac{3}{10} =$

8. $*\frac{2}{3} - \frac{1}{4} =$

*NOTE: In this case, we have to change both denominators to make like denominators. Start by finding the **least common denominator**, the smallest number that is a multiple of both 3 and 4. The least common denominator of 3 and 4 is 12. To change both fractions so that their denominator becomes 12, do this:

$$\frac{2}{3} \times \frac{4}{4} = \frac{8}{12}$$

$$\frac{1}{4} \times \frac{3}{3} = \frac{3}{12}$$

Now can you solve it?

Reteaching Math: Fractions and Decimals © 2008 by Bob Krech, Scholastic Teaching Resources

Name: _____ Date: _____

Adding and Subtracting Fractions
with Unlike Denominators

Add. Simplify your answers.

1. $\frac{3}{16} + \frac{3}{8} =$

2. $\frac{1}{3} + \frac{5}{12} =$

3. $\frac{1}{10} + \frac{1}{5} =$

4. $\frac{2}{8} + \frac{1}{4} =$

5. $\frac{1}{4} + \frac{5}{12} =$

6. $\frac{3}{8} + \frac{2}{4} =$

Subtract. Simplify your answers.

7. $\frac{5}{10} - \frac{1}{5} =$

8. $\frac{7}{12} - \frac{2}{4} =$

9. $\frac{4}{8} - \frac{1}{2} =$

10. $\frac{3}{4} - \frac{1}{2} =$

11. $\frac{4}{16} - \frac{1}{8} =$

12. $\frac{7}{9} - \frac{1}{3} =$

Review:

13. Write $\frac{7}{4}$ as a whole or mixed number. _____

14. Write $1\frac{4}{6}$ as an improper fraction. _____

15. Make these fractions equivalent: $\frac{2}{3} = \frac{12}{}$

16. a. What is the denominator in $\frac{3}{4}$? _____ b. What does it mean? _____

Name: _____   Date: _____

Pieces of Fruit-O Bars

Directions: Customers who don't want a whole Fruit-O Bar are ordering pieces of Fruit-O Bars. Here are the notes from yesterday's orders. Fill in the flavor chart to help the candy makers decide how much to make of each flavor.

Orders		
$\frac{3}{4}$ cherry	$\frac{1}{2}$ orange	$\frac{1}{3}$ grape
$\frac{1}{4}$ lime	$\frac{1}{4}$ lime	$\frac{1}{8}$ lemon
$\frac{1}{2}$ orange	$\frac{1}{4}$ lime	$\frac{1}{8}$ lemon
$\frac{1}{2}$ orange	$\frac{3}{4}$ cherry	$\frac{2}{3}$ blueberry
$\frac{3}{4}$ cherry	$\frac{1}{2}$ orange	$\frac{1}{8}$ lemon
$\frac{1}{4}$ lime	$\frac{3}{4}$ cherry	$\frac{2}{3}$ blueberry
$\frac{3}{4}$ cherry	$\frac{1}{2}$ orange	$\frac{1}{8}$ lemon

Flavor Chart		
Flavor	**Multiplication Calculation**	**Total Bars Ordered**
Cherry		
Orange		
Grape		
Lemon		
Blueberry		
Lime		

Reteaching Math: Fractions and Decimals © 2008 by Bob Krech, Scholastic Teaching Resources

Name: _____ Date: _____

Bev found $\frac{1}{4}$ of a gold bar. Her cousin Bart helped her find it so she is going to give Bart $\frac{1}{2}$. How much of a full gold bar will Bart get?

BASICS BOX

In this problem, we need to find $\frac{1}{2}$ of $\frac{1}{4}$ (of a gold bar). *Of* is the key word here. We sometimes use *of* to describe multiplying. For example, 3 x 5 can be described as 3 sets of 5. So to solve Bev and Bart's problem, we need to multiply $\frac{1}{2}$ by $\frac{1}{4}$:

1. Multiply the numerators and denominators:

$$\frac{1}{2} \times \frac{1}{4} = \frac{1}{8}$$

2. Reduce and simplify if possible. (In this case, $\frac{1}{8}$ is already in simplest form.)

$$\frac{1}{2} \text{ of } \frac{1}{4} \text{ is } \frac{1}{8}$$

Bart gets $\frac{1}{8}$ of a gold bar.

JOURNAL

Linda has run $\frac{7}{16}$ of a mile so far. She is supposed to run $\frac{7}{8}$ of a mile. Her coach yells, "Linda, you're halfway there!" Is the coach right? Prove your answer using words, numbers, and pictures.

PRACTICE

Find the products.

1. $\frac{1}{4} \times \frac{1}{8} =$

2. $\frac{2}{3} \times \frac{1}{3} =$

3. $\frac{1}{3} \times \frac{2}{5} =$

4. $\frac{1}{4} \times \frac{1}{4} =$

5. $\frac{2}{3} \times \frac{1}{7} =$

6. $\frac{1}{4} \times \frac{1}{3} =$

7. $\frac{2}{3} \times \frac{1}{6} =$

8. *3 $\times \frac{1}{2} =$

9. 8 $\times \frac{3}{4} =$

10. **3$\frac{1}{4} \times \frac{1}{3} =$

* NOTE: To multiply fractions and whole numbers, change the whole number into a fraction first. So, 3 becomes $\frac{3}{1}$.

** HINT: Change the mixed number to an improper fraction first.

Name: _____   Date: _____

Multiplying Fractions

Multiply. Simplify your answers.

1. $\frac{1}{3} \times \frac{1}{6} =$

2. $\frac{1}{2} \times \frac{1}{8} =$

3. $\frac{3}{5} \times \frac{2}{3} =$

4. $\frac{3}{4} \times \frac{8}{16} =$

5. $\frac{1}{8} \times \frac{1}{8} =$

6. $2\frac{7}{8} \times \frac{1}{4} =$

7. $9 \times \frac{1}{3} =$

8. $\frac{1}{4} \times 16 =$

9. $\frac{1}{2} \times 8 =$

10. $5 \times \frac{1}{2} =$

11. $\frac{2}{3} \times 21 =$

12. $2 \times \frac{7}{8} =$

Review:

13. $\frac{1}{8} + \frac{2}{8} =$

14. $\frac{5}{9} - \frac{3}{9} =$

15. $\frac{1}{2} + \frac{1}{4} =$

16. $\frac{3}{8} + \frac{1}{4} =$

17. $\frac{3}{8} - \frac{1}{4} =$

18. $\frac{14}{16} - \frac{7}{8} =$

19. Write this improper fraction as a mixed number: $\frac{24}{16} =$

20. Circle the fraction in simplest form:

$$\frac{2}{3} \qquad \frac{4}{16} \qquad \frac{2}{4}$$

Reteaching Math: Fractions and Decimals © 2008 by Bob Krech, Scholastic Teaching Resources

Name: _____   Date: _____

Reteaching Math: Fractions and Decimals © 2008 by Bob Krech, Scholastic Teaching Resources

WORD PROBLEM

Ronald has $\frac{1}{2}$ yard of licorice string. How many $\frac{1}{8}$-yard pieces can he cut that into?

BASICS BOX

In Ronald's problem, we want to find out how many eighths make up a half. To find out how many of a fraction makes up another fraction, we divide fractions by fractions:

$$\frac{1}{2} \div \frac{1}{8} = ?$$

1. Invert (or flip) the divisor, so $\frac{1}{8}$ becomes $\frac{8}{1}$

$$\frac{1}{2} \div \frac{8}{1} = ?$$

2. Multiply the numerators and denominators

$$\frac{1}{2} \times \frac{8}{1} = \frac{8}{2}$$

3. Reduce to simplest form

$\frac{8}{2} = 4$ pieces that are $\frac{1}{8}$ yard long

EXAMPLE

Jill has 8 inches of gold wire. How many $\frac{1}{4}$-inch pinky rings can she make?

$$8 \div \frac{1}{4} = ?$$

* If you're dividing whole numbers and fractions, change the whole number into a fraction first. In this case, 8 becomes $\frac{8}{1}$.

$$\frac{8}{1} \div \frac{1}{4} = ?$$

$$\frac{8}{1} \times \frac{4}{1} = \frac{32}{1}$$

32 pinky rings

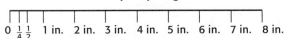

Can you figure it out another way using this picture?

PRACTICE

Find the quotients.

1. $\frac{1}{2} \div \frac{1}{16} =$

2. $\frac{1}{10} \div \frac{1}{10} =$

3. $\frac{2}{6} \div \frac{1}{3} =$

4. $\frac{7}{8} \div \frac{1}{4} =$

5. $\frac{1}{3} \div \frac{1}{9} =$

6. $\frac{12}{16} \div \frac{1}{8} =$

7. $\frac{1}{2} \div \frac{1}{4} =$

8. $\frac{2}{4} \div \frac{1}{4} =$

9. $2 \div \frac{1}{6} =$

10. $6 \div \frac{1}{4} =$

JOURNAL

Draw a picture to show how to find $\frac{3}{4} \div \frac{1}{2}$.

Name: _____   Date: _____

Dividing Fractions by Fractions

Divide. Simplify your answers.

1. $\dfrac{1}{2} \div \dfrac{1}{8} =$

2. $\dfrac{7}{8} \div \dfrac{1}{4} =$

3. $\dfrac{1}{3} \div \dfrac{1}{2} =$

4. $\dfrac{2}{9} \div \dfrac{1}{16} =$

5. $\dfrac{3}{4} \div \dfrac{3}{8} =$

6. $\dfrac{7}{8} \div \dfrac{1}{16} =$

7. $8 \div \dfrac{1}{4} =$

8. $16 \div \dfrac{1}{2} =$

9. $12 \div \dfrac{1}{4} =$

10. $10 \div \dfrac{2}{5} =$

11. $3 \div \dfrac{1}{3} =$

12. $16 \div \dfrac{1}{8} =$

Review:

13. $10 \times \dfrac{1}{2} =$

14. $\dfrac{1}{4} \times \dfrac{3}{8} =$

15. $\dfrac{5}{8} \times \dfrac{1}{3} =$

16. $\dfrac{1}{2} - \dfrac{1}{2} =$

17. $\dfrac{5}{8} - \dfrac{4}{8} =$

18. $\dfrac{7}{8} + \dfrac{1}{4} =$

19. $\dfrac{7}{16} - \dfrac{1}{3} =$

Make these fractions equivalent.

20. $\dfrac{10}{100} = \dfrac{1}{}$

21. $\dfrac{}{16} = \dfrac{1}{8}$

22. $\dfrac{7}{24} = \dfrac{}{48}$

Reteaching Math: Fractions and Decimals © 2008 by Bob Krech, Scholastic Teaching Resources

Name: _____   Date: _____

The Super-Sour Square

Place Value Chart						
Thousands	Hundreds	Tens	Ones		tenths	hundredths
				.		

Name: _____ Date: _____

Super-Sour Square Order Form #1

Order 1: I would like one Super-Sour Square, please. Please make $\frac{1}{10}$ of it orange and the rest lime.

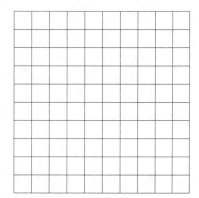

Flavor	Fraction	Decimal

Order 2: Could I have a Super-Sour Square that's $\frac{1}{2}$ lemon and $\frac{1}{2}$ cherry? Thank you.

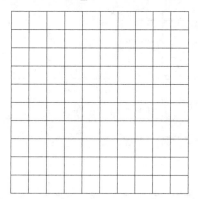

Flavor	Fraction	Decimal

Order 3: Could I have a Super-Sour Square, please? I would like $\frac{6}{10}$ lemon and the rest blueberry. Thank you very much!

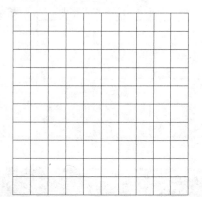

Flavor	Fraction	Decimal

Order 4: Please make me one Super-Sour Square. How about $\frac{3}{10}$ cherry, $\frac{3}{10}$ lemon, and the rest orange? Thank you.

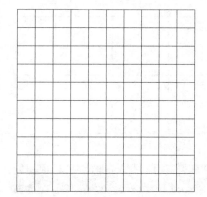

Flavor	Fraction	Decimal

Reteaching Math: Fractions and Decimals © 2008 by Bob Krech, Scholastic Teaching Resources

Name: _____ Date: _____

Fraction/Decimal Matching Game (Directions)

Materials: Fraction and Decimal cards (p. 78)　　　Players: 2

1. Shuffle the deck and place four cards face up between the two players. Then deal out the remainder of the deck to the two players.

2. Players look at their cards to see if any of them are equivalent. For example, if a player has a 1/2 card and a 0.5 card, those cards are equivalent. Players put down their equivalent cards in their own match piles.

3. Next, players take turns looking to see if any of their cards have an equivalent card on the table. For example, if there is a 3/10 card on the table and a player has a 0.3 card, those cards are equivalent.

4. If a player finds a match, she picks up the card from the table and places it in her match pile. A player can make as many matches as possible during a turn. When no match is possible, the player must put down a card on the table.

5. Play continues until both players have used up all their cards. The player with the most cards in her match pile wins.

Reteaching Math: Fractions and Decimals © 2008 by Bob Krech, Scholastic Teaching Resources

77

Name: _____ Date: _____

Fraction/Decimal Matching Game (Cards)

Cut out the cards below.

$\frac{1}{4}$	0.25	$\frac{1}{2}$	0.5	$\frac{3}{4}$
0.75	$\frac{1}{10}$	0.1	$\frac{2}{10}$	0.2
$\frac{3}{10}$	0.3	$\frac{4}{10}$	0.4	$\frac{5}{10}$
0.5	$\frac{6}{10}$	0.6	$\frac{7}{10}$	0.7
$\frac{8}{10}$	0.8	$\frac{9}{10}$	0.9	$\frac{1}{5}$
0.2	$\frac{2}{5}$	0.4	$\frac{3}{5}$	0.6

Reteaching Math: Fractions and Decimals © 2008 by Bob Krech, Scholastic Teaching Resources

Name: _____ Date: _____

Jordan wanted half a dollar from the coin machine. She tried typing in $\frac{1}{2}$ on the keypad, but it only accepted decimal amounts. What should she type in to get the half dollar?

BASICS BOX

Like fractions, decimals talk about pieces of a whole. We can say $\frac{1}{4}$ with fractions or 0.25 with decimals—they're exactly the same amount. In Jordan's case, she wants $\frac{1}{2}$ of a dollar, which is 50 cents or 50/100 of a dollar. She should type 0.50, the decimal equivalent of $\frac{50}{100}$. We usually write about money using decimals. Here is a place value chart that includes decimals and whole numbers.

Place Value Chart						
Thousands	Hundreds	Tens	Ones	.	tenths	hundredths
			0	.	5	

The decimal point separates whole numbers from decimals.

PRACTICE

1. $\frac{1}{10}$ = ◯ =

2. $\frac{2}{10}$ = ◯ =

3. $\frac{3}{10}$ = ◯ =

4. ◯ = 0.4 =

5. $\frac{5}{10}$ = ◯ =

6. ◯ = 0.6 =

7. ◯ = ◯ =

8. ◯ = ◯ =

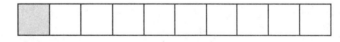
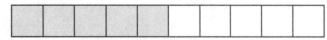

JOURNAL

Ralph said $\frac{9}{10}$ of his marble collection is blue. The rest is red. Draw a picture of his collection and label with decimals.

Reteaching Math: Fractions and Decimals © 2008 by Bob Krech, Scholastic Teaching Resources

Name: _____ Date: _____

Introducing Decimals

Fill in the blanks.

1. 0.9 = _____ tenths

2. _____ = six tenths

3. $\frac{3}{10}$ = 0. _____

4. $\frac{2}{10}$ = 0. _____

5. 0.8 = $\frac{}{10}$

6. 0.1 = $\frac{}{10}$

Match the fraction with the decimal.

7. $\frac{1}{2}$ =   0.7

8. $\frac{7}{10}$ =   0.5

9. $\frac{4}{10}$ =   0.5

10. $\frac{5}{10}$ =   0.4

Fill in the blanks with a decimal.

11. $\frac{3}{10}$ of a Fruit-O Bar was orange.
    The rest was cherry. How much was

    cherry? _____

12. 0.8 of a Super-Sour Square was grape.

    The rest was lemon. How much was

    lemon? _____

13. Color in 0.9 of the Super-Sour
    Square green.

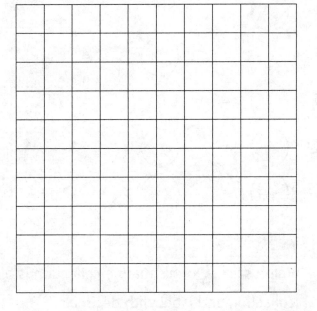

Reteaching Math: Fractions and Decimals © 2008 by Bob Krech, Scholastic Teaching Resources

Name: _____   Date: _____

Super-Sour Square Order Form #2

Order 1:

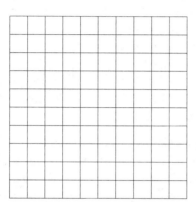

Flavor	Fraction	Decimal

Order 2:

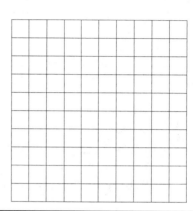

Flavor	Fraction	Decimal

Order 3:

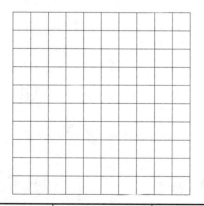

Flavor	Fraction	Decimal

Order 4:

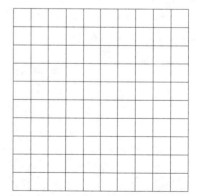

Flavor	Fraction	Decimal

Name: _____ Date: _____

The Squeeze Game – Decimal Version

Materials: Decimal cards (below)   Players: 2

1. Place the 0 card at one end of a desk and the 1 card at the other end. Place the 0.5 card right in the middle of the 0 and 1 cards.

2. Shuffle the decimal cards. Deal six cards to each player.

3. Players take turns placing a card so it touches either side of another card on the desk. Cards must be placed in increasing order. A card may not be placed between two other touching cards.

4. The object of the game is to place as many cards as you can. A round is over when a player can no longer place any of his or her cards. The number of cards left in a player's hands is his or her score.

5. At the end of a round, return any leftover cards to the deck and shuffle. Repeat steps 1 to 4 to play another round.

6. After six rounds, add up players' points. The player with the least number of points wins.

Cut out the cards below.			
0	1	0.1	0.2
0.3	0.4	0.5	0.6
0.7	0.8	0.35	0.9
0.55	0.25	0.85	0.95
0.05	0.15	0.45	0.65

Reteaching Math: Fractions and Decimals © 2008 by Bob Krech, Scholastic Teaching Resources

Name: _____ Date: _____

Charlie loves nuts—the more the better. Which bag should he choose to get the most nuts?

A.
0.02 lbs

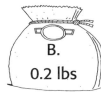
B.
0.2 lbs

C.
0.29 lbs

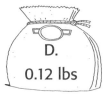
D.
0.12 lbs

BASICS BOX

When comparing decimals, make sure the decimal points are lined up. For Charlie's bags we could compare the bag weights like this:
A. 0.02
B. 0.2
C. 0.29
D. 0.12

Start with the whole numbers if there are any. Move from left to right. For Charlie, we see the ones are the same (0) so we move to the tenths place. Bag A has 0 tenths and Bag D has 1 tenths. These are smaller than Bags B and C, which have 2 tenths. We then move right to the hundredths place. Bag B has 0 hundredths, while C has 9 hundredths. So Bag C weighs more. Charlie should choose Bag C.

PRACTICE

Write <, >, or = to complete the number sentence.

1. 0.5 ◯ 0.50
2. 6.31 ◯ 6.09
3. 0.2 ◯ 0.5
4. 1.2 ◯ 1.3

5. 0.99 ◯ 1.01
6. 7.70 ◯ 7.7
7. 5.11 ◯ 4.90
8. 3.6 ◯ 6.3

Put these numbers in order from smallest to largest.

9. 2.89 2.47 2.98 2.06
____ ____ ____ ____

10. 9.05 5.09 9.50 59.0
____ ____ ____ ____

11. 0.32 3.20 3.33 0.93
____ ____ ____ ____

12. 0.17 0.07 0.01 0.09
____ ____ ____ ____

JOURNAL

Compare 0.51 and 0.05. Which is larger? Draw a diagram or picture of each number to support your answer.

Name: _____ Date: _____

Comparing and Ordering Decimals

Circle the larger number.

1. 0.25 or 0.10

2. 0.7 or 0.8

3. 0.5 or 0.25

4. 0.12 or 1.2

5. 1.3 or 0.13

6. 0.90 or 1.04

Put these numbers in order from smallest to largest.

7. 0.45   0.10   0.25   0.15   _____ _____ _____ _____

8. 6.10   10.6   0.160   1.0   _____ _____ _____ _____

9. 1.8   1.1   1.07   1.71   _____ _____ _____ _____

10. 0.9   0.3   0.2   0.1   _____ _____ _____ _____

Write the fraction as a decimal.

11. $\dfrac{4}{10} =$

12. $\dfrac{40}{100} =$

13. $\dfrac{25}{100} =$

Write the decimal as a fraction.

14. 0.10 = _____

15. 0.75 = _____

16. 0.90 = _____

Review:

17. $\dfrac{1}{4} \times \dfrac{1}{4} =$

18. $\dfrac{3}{8} \times \dfrac{1}{3} =$

19. $\dfrac{1}{2} \div \dfrac{1}{4} =$

20. $\dfrac{5}{16} + \dfrac{1}{16} =$

21. $\dfrac{7}{8} + \dfrac{3}{4} =$

22. $1 - \dfrac{3}{4} =$

Reteaching Math: Fractions and Decimals © 2008 by Bob Krech, Scholastic Teaching Resources

Name: _____ Date: _____

Multiple Super-Sour Square Order Form

Square #1:

Flavor	Fraction	Decimal
Lemon		
Orange		
Cherry		
Lime		
Grape		
Blueberry		
Total		

Square #2:

Flavor	Fraction	Decimal
Lemon		
Orange		
Cherry		
Lime		
Grape		
Blueberry		
Total		

Square #3:

Flavor	Fraction	Decimal
Lemon		
Orange		
Cherry		
Lime		
Grape		
Blueberry		
Total		

Order Totals

						Fraction	Decimal

Reteaching Math: Fractions and Decimals © 2008 by Bob Krech, Scholastic Teaching Resources

PRACTICE PAGE #12

Name: _____   Date: _____

WORD PROBLEM

Beth had 0.75 pounds of grapes. She bought another 0.25 pounds.
How many pounds of grapes does she have now?

BASICS BOX

To find out about Beth's grapes, we
have to add decimals:

1. Line up the decimal points, including
   the decimal point for the sum.

   0.75
   + 0.25
   .

2. Add from right to left, as you would
   with whole numbers. Regroup as
   needed.

   0.75
   + 0.25
   1.00

   1.00 pound of grapes

If Beth had 0.75 pounds of grapes and
ate 0.25 pounds, how much would be
left? Here we subtract.

1. Line up decimal points, including the
   decimal point for the difference.

   0.75
   − 0.25
   .

2. Subtract from left to right, as you
   would with whole numbers. Regroup
   as needed.

   0.75
   − 0.25
   0.50

   0.50 pounds of grapes left

PRACTICE

Solve these problems.

1. $10.50 + 8.25 =$ _____

2. $9.08 + 4.52 =$ _____

3. $3.12 - 1.41 =$ _____

4. $0.03 + 0.01 =$ _____

5. $8.41 - 0.39 =$ _____

6. $212.1 + 16.9 =$ _____

7. $3.00 + 2.36 =$ _____

8. $44.22 - 15.88 =$ _____

9. $0.192 + 0.618 =$ _____

10. $3.75 +$ _____ $= 4.66$

11. $9.2 - 1.55 =$ _____

12. $6.15 + 3.9 =$ _____

JOURNAL

Tell how you would find the sum of 16.25 and
9.9. Use pictures, words, and numbers. Then
explain how you would find the difference
between the two numbers.

Reteaching Math: Fractions and Decimals © 2008 by Bob Krech, Scholastic Teaching Resources

Name: _____   Date: _____

Adding and Subtracting Decimals

Solve.

1. $0.25 - 0.10 =$ _____

2. $0.02 + 0.01 =$ _____

3. $5.12 + 3.22 =$ _____

4. $50.00 - 1.35 =$ _____

5. $9.41 + 0.05 =$ _____

6. $8.25 - 2.35 =$ _____

7. $\$7.95 + \$3.95 =$ _____

8. $0.61 - 0.59 =$ _____

9. $4.15 - 2.2 =$ _____

10. $127.3 - 12.6 =$ _____

11. $\$1.05 + \$0.44 =$ _____

12. $8.43 - 0.09 =$ _____

13. $1.00 - 0.90 =$ _____

14. $0.88 + 0.88 =$ _____

Review:

Write each decimal as a fraction.

15. $0.25 =$ _____

16. $0.55 =$ _____

17. $0.60 =$ _____

Write each fraction as a decimal.

18. $\dfrac{50}{100} =$ _____

19. $\dfrac{1}{4} =$ _____

20. $\dfrac{3}{10} =$ _____

Solve.

21. $\dfrac{1}{2} + \dfrac{1}{4} =$

22. $\dfrac{1}{2} - \dfrac{1}{4} =$

23. $\dfrac{1}{2} \times \dfrac{1}{4} =$

Name: _____ Date: _____

Pieces of Super-Sour Squares

The Fabulously Fruity Candy Company has lots of leftover pieces of Super-Sour Squares. They plan on combining these to make full-size Super-Sour Squares. For example, they found 9 leftover pieces of lemon. Each pieces was 0.25 of a full Super-Sour Square. If they put them together, how many new squares could they make?

$$0.25 \times 9 = 2.25 \text{ Super-Sour Squares}$$

Directions: Complete the form below.

Number of Pieces	Size of Pieces	Computation	How Many Super-Sour Squares?
4 Orange	0.25		
5 Grape	0.25		
5 Cherry	0.50		
7 Blueberry	0.75		
100 Lemon	0.6		
50 Lime	0.01		
10 Cherry	0.35		
3 Grape	0.9		

Bonus: Choose one of the examples above. Using graph paper, show that your computation is correct.

Reteaching Math: Fractions and Decimals © 2008 by Bob Krech, Scholastic Teaching Resources

Name: _____   Date: _____

Melvin bought 2.5 pounds of dog chow for his puppy, Goliath.
Dog chow costs $3.12 a pound. How much did Melvin spend?

BASICS BOX

Multiplying decimals is basically the same as multiplying whole numbers. The only difference is that you have to correctly place a decimal point in the product.

$$\begin{array}{r} \$3.12 \\ \times 2.50 \\ \hline 1560 \\ 6240 \\ \hline 7800 \end{array}$$

To place the decimal point correctly, count the places to the right of the decimal point in both factors: 3.12 and 2.5. In this case, it's three. This will be the number of places to the right of the decimal point in the product.

7.800

Melvin spent $7.80.

JOURNAL

Jinx said that 3.5 x 0.5 = 17.5.
Is she correct? Why or why not? Support your answer with pictures, words, and numbers.

PRACTICE

Find the products.

1. $41.5 \times 3 =$ _____

2. $0.24 \times 9 =$ _____

3. $2.4 \times 1.2 =$ _____

4. $1.5 \times 4.3 =$ _____

5. $0.02 \times 0.01 =$ _____

6. $31.2 \times 0.9 =$ _____

7. $112 \times 4.1 =$ _____

8. $3.0 \times 0.5 =$ _____

9. $0.25 \times 9 =$ _____

10. $0.1 \times 0.1 =$ _____

*You may notice that when a whole number is multiplied by a decimal, the product is smaller than the whole number. Remember, we are multiplying the whole number by something less than 1. Another way to look at it is that we are taking something less than 1 and multiplying it several times, like: $3 \times 0.25 = 0.25 + 0.25 + 0.25 = 0.75$

Name: _____ Date: _____

Multiplying Decimals

1. $\$5.41 \times 4 =$ _____

2. $0.50 \times 5 =$ _____

3. $3.3 \times 3.3 =$ _____

4. $0.05 \times 0.07 =$ _____

5. $163 \times 8.4 =$ _____

6. $11.6 \times 9 =$ _____

7. $\$3.89 \times 2 =$ _____

8. $0.07 \times 0.03 =$ _____

9. $21 \times 0.5 =$ _____

10. $250 \times 0.10 =$ _____

Review:

11. $347 - 1.08 =$ _____

12. $52.4 + 36.19 =$ _____

Reduce these fractions to simplest form.

13. $\frac{4}{32} =$

14. $\frac{10}{100} =$

15. $\frac{4}{16} =$

Solve:

16. $\frac{4}{5} - \frac{2}{5} =$

17. $\frac{1}{3} \times 7 =$

18. $14 \div \frac{1}{4} =$

Reteaching Math: Fractions and Decimals © 2008 by Bob Krech, Scholastic Teaching Resources

Name: _____ Date: _____

Super-Sour Squares Special Order Form

Directions: Here are some Super-Sour Squares that have been special-ordered and need to be shared. Suggest to each customer how each order should be shared. Use division to help you find an accurate answer.

Super-Sour Square Ordered	Number of People Sharing	Computation	Amount of Square per Person
Orange 1.5 squares	3		
Grape 2.75 squares	25		
Cherry 0.5 squares	2		
Blueberry 10.25 squares	5		
Lemon 8.01 squares	6		
Lime 12.2 squares	5		
Cherry 3.9 squares	10		
Grape 31.5 squares	100		

Bonus: Choose one of the examples above. Using graph paper, show that your computation is correct.

Reteaching Math: Fractions and Decimals © 2008 by Bob Krech, Scholastic Teaching Resources

Name: _____ Date: _____

WORD PROBLEM

Zammo had 8.2 pounds of Stinkmeister cheese. He wanted to share it with Larry, Barry, and Harry. How much cheese should each boy get?

BASICS BOX

To help Zammo, we will have to divide the 8.2 pounds of cheese evenly 4 ways:

1. Set up the division problem as you would with whole numbers.

$$4\overline{)8.2}$$

2. Place the decimal point in the quotient above the decimal point in the dividend.

$$4\overline{)8.2}^{\,.}$$

3. Divide.

```
      2.05
  4)8.2
    8
    0 2
      0
      20
      20
```

2.05 pounds of cheese for each boy

PRACTICE

Find the quotients.

1. $2\overline{)17.2}$

2. $5\overline{)32.5}$

3. $3\overline{)2.67}$

4. $4\overline{)107.2}$

5. $3\overline{)267.3}$

6. $8\overline{)24.992}$

7. $9\overline{)5.22}$

8. $13\overline{)3.12}$

9. $44\overline{)46.64}$

10. $4\overline{)17.8}$

JOURNAL

Write a word problem that uses the numbers 6 and 2.4 and requires division to solve. Solve it and show your thinking.

Reteaching Math: Fractions and Decimals © 2008 by Bob Krech, Scholastic Teaching Resources

Name: _____ Date: _____

Dividing Decimals

1. $3\overline{)9.6}$

2. $4\overline{)12.8}$

3. $5\overline{)1.00}$

4. $2\overline{)251.8}$

5. $8\overline{)3.24}$

6. $12\overline{)24.24}$

7. $35\overline{)222.25}$

8. $11\overline{)22.22}$

9. $5\overline{)0.02}$

Review:

10. $0.25 \times 6 =$ _____

11. $0.04 \times 0.12 =$ _____

12. $182 \times .54 =$ _____

13. $1.15 + 3.03 =$ _____

14. $0.02 + 0.99 =$ _____

15. $5.43 - 0.28 =$ _____

16. $\frac{2}{3} - \frac{1}{4} =$

17. $\frac{5}{7} + \frac{3}{5} =$

18. $\frac{3}{4} \div \frac{1}{16} =$

19. Write as a mixed number:

$\frac{27}{12} =$

20. How much is $\frac{1}{5}$ of 100? _____

Practice Page #1 (p. 39)
Clay fractions will vary.
Journal: Answers will vary.

Review Page #1 (p. 40)
1. 1/2
2. 1/4
3. 3/4
4. 8, 1
5. No; because although it is cut in four pieces, they are not equal pieces.
6. 1/3
7. 3/8
8. 1/4
9. 1/2
10. 5/16

Practice Page #2 (p. 43)
1. 1/2
2. 3/8
3. 1/9
4. 1/3
5. 1/4
6. 3/4
7. 2/3
8. 1/6
9. Answers will vary.
10. Answers will vary.
Journal: Pictures will vary.

Review Page #2 (p. 44)
1. to 7. Drawings will vary.
8. 2/3
9. 1/4
10. 3/8
11. 7
12. 10
13. 2/3

Practice Page #3 (p. 48)
1. 1/2 = 2/4 = 3/6 = 4/8 = 5/10 = 6/12
2. 1/4 = 2/8 = 3/12
3. 1/3 = 2/6 = 4/12
4. 2/5 = 4/10
5. 2/3 = 4/6 = 8/12
6. 1/6 = 2/12
7. 3/4 = 6/8 = 9/12
Journal: Yes; explanations will vary.

Review Page #3 (p. 49)
Numbers 3, 4, 6, and 7 should be circled.
9. 8
10. 2
11. 18
12. 8
13. 2
14. 16
15. 8
16. 3

17. Answers will vary.
18. 3/8
19. 5/8
20. 2/6 or 1/3
21. 3
22. 8

Practice Page #4 (p. 52)
1. 6
2. 5
3. 12
4. 15
5. 4
6. 10
Journal: 25; methods for finding the answer will vary.

Review Page #4 (p. 53)
1. 1/4
2. 2/4 or 1/2
3. 1/2
4. 5/6
5. 2/5
6. 3/8
7. 4/5
8. 3/9
9. 1/5
10. 1/2
11. 8
12. 4
13. 1/4
14. 2
15. 1
16. 16
17. 3/8
18. 7/8

Practice Page #5 (p. 56)
1. 1/5
2. 1/2
3. 3/7
4. 4/5
5. circled
6. 1/4
7. 3/4
8. 3/4
9. circled
10. 3/5
11. 5/12
12. 1/4
13. 2/9
14. 8/10
15. 3/18, 1/2, 6/9
16. 2/10, 3/5, 16/20
Journal: 2/3; methods for finding the answer will vary.

Review Page #5 (p. 57)
1. 3/4
2. 1/2
3. 1/2
4. 3/4
5. 5/6
6. 1/5
7. 1/4
8. 1/4
9. 1/16
10. 7/8
11. 2/3
12. 3/8
13. 14/16
14. 4/12
15. 3/16, 1/4, 7/16, 1/2
16. 3/10, 3/8, 3/5, 3/4
17. 1/8, 1/2, 2/3, 3/4

Practice Page #6 (p. 60)
1. 3/4
2. 3/4
3. 6/7
4. 0
5. 1/16
6. 1/2
7. 3/3 or 1
8. 1/5
9. 1/3
10. 3/16
Journal: 2/3; methods for finding the answer will vary.

Review Page #6 (p. 61)
1. 3/4
2. 5/6
3. 1/2
4. 1
5. 7/16
6. 4/5
7. 1/5
8. 1/4
9. 1/4
10. 5/16
11. 2/9
12. 1/3
13. 4/5
14. 1/4
15. 1
16. 7/8
17. 0
18. 4/7

Practice Page #7 (p. 64)
1. 1-2/3
2. 2
3. 3-1/2
4. 2-1/4
5. 1
6. 8/3

7. 3/2
8. 7/2
9. 7/4
10. 17/8
11. <
12. <
13. <
Journal: 9/6 = 1-1/2; 1-4/5 = 9/5;
methods for finding the answer will vary.

Review Page #7 (p. 65)
1. 2
2. 1
3. 4
4. 2-1/2
5. 1-3/7
6. 1-1/3
7. 5/4
8. 11/5
9. 8/5
10. 18/7
11. 10/3
12. 17/10
13. 2/3
14. 4/5
15. 3/8
16. 4
17. 1/8, 3/16, 1/2, 3/4

Practice Page #8 (p. 68)
1. 5/8
2. 9/10
3. 5/6
4. 7/8
5. 1/4
6. 2/9
7. 1/2
8. 5/12
Journal: Answers will vary.

Review Page #8 (p. 69)
1. 9/16
2. 3/4
3. 3/10
4. 1/2
5. 2/3
6. 7/8
7. 3/10
8. 1/12
9. 0
10. 1/4
11. 1/8
12. 4/9
13. 1-3/4
14. 10/6 or 5/3
15. 18
16. a. 4;
 b. The number of equal parts the
 fraction has

Pieces of Fruit-O Bars (p. 70)
Cherry – 3-3/4 bars
Orange – 2-1/2 bars
Grape – 1/3 bar
Lemon – 1/2 bar
Blueberry – 1-1/3 bars
Lime – 1 bar

Practice Page #9A (p. 71)
1. 1/32
2. 2/9
3. 2/15
4. 1/16
5. 2/21
6. 1/12
7. 1/9
8. 1-1/2
9. 6
10. 1-1/12
Journal: Yes; explanations will vary.

Review Page #9A (p. 72)
1. 1/18
2. 1/16
3. 2/5
4. 3/8
5. 1/64
6. 23/32
7. 3
8. 4
9. 4
10. 2-1/2
11. 14
12. 1-3/4
13. 3/8
14. 2/9
15. 3/4
16. 5/8
17. 1/8
18. 0
19. 1-1/2
20. 2/3

Practice Page #9B (p. 73)
1. 8
2. 1
3. 1
4. 3-1/2
5. 3
6. 6
7. 2
8. 2
9. 12
10. 24
Journal: 1-1/2; pictures will vary.

Review Page #9B (p. 74)
1. 4
2. 3-1/2
3. 2/3
4. 3-5/9
5. 2
6. 56
7. 32
8. 32
9. 48
10. 25
11. 9
12. 128
13. 5
14. 3/32
15. 5/24
16. 0
17. 1/8
18. 1-1/8
19. 5/48
20. 10
21. 2
22. 14

Practice Page #10 (p. 79)
1. 0.1
2. 0.2
3. 0.3
4. 4/10
5. 0.5
6. 6/10
7. 7/10; 0.7
8. 8/10; 0.8
Journal: 0.9 blue; 0.1 red

Review Page #10 (p. 80)
1. 9
2. 6/10 or 0.6
3. 3
4. 2
5. 8
6. 1
7. 0.5
8. 0.7
9. 0.4
10. 0.5
11. 0.7
12. 0.2
13. Color square as per directions

Practice Page #11 (p. 83)
1. =
2. >
3. <
4. <
5. <
6. =
7. >
8. <
9. 2.06, 2.47, 2.89, 2.98

95

10. 5.09, 9.05, 9.50, 59.0
11. 0.32, 0.93, 3.20, 3.33
12. 0.01, 0.07, 0.09, 0.17
Journal: 0.51; diagrams or pictures will vary.

Review Page #11 (p. 84)
1. 0.25
2. 0.8
3. 0.5
4. 1.2
5. 1.3
6. 1.04
7. 0.10, 0.15, 0.25, 0.45
8. 0.160, 1.0, 6.10, 10.6
9. 1.07, 1.1, 1.71, 1.8
10. 0.1, 0.2, 0.3, 0.9
11. 0.4
12. 0.40
13. 0.25
14. 1/10
15. 3/4 or 75/100
16. 90/100 or 9/10
17. 1/16
18. 1/8
19. 2
20. 3/8
21. 1-5/8
22. 1/4

Practice Page #12 (p. 86)
1. 18.75
2. 13.60
3. 1.71
4. 0.04
5. 8.02
6. 229.0
7. 5.36
8. 28.34
9. 0.810
10. 0.91
11. 7.65
12. 10.05
Journal: 26.15; explanations will vary.

Review Page #12 (p. 87)
1. 0.15
2. 0.03
3. 8.34
4. 48.65
5. 9.46
6. 5.90
7. $11.90
8. 0.02
9. 1.95
10. 114.7
11. $1.49
12. 8.34
13. 0.10
14. 1.76

15. 1/4
16. 55/100
17. 60/100 or 6/10 or 3/5
18. 0.50
19. 0.25
20. 0.3
21. 3/4
22. 1/4
23. 1/8

Pieces of Super-Sour Squares (p. 88)
Orange: 4 × 0.25 = 1
Grape: 5 × 0.25 = 1.25
Cherry: 5 × 0.50 = 2.5
Blueberry: 7 × 0.75 = 5.25
Lemon: 100 × 0.6 = 60
Lime: 50 × 0.01 = 0.5
Cherry: 10 × 0.35 = 3.5
Grape: 3 × 0.9 = 2.7

Practice Page #13 (p. 89)
1. 124.5
2. 2.16
3. 2.88
4. 6.45
5. 0.0002
6. 28.08
7. 459.2
8. 1.5
9. 2.25
10. 0.01
Journal: No; explanations will vary.

Review Page #13 (p. 90)
1. $21.64
2. 2.50
3. 10.89
4. 0.0035
5. 1,369.2
6. 104.4
7. $7.78
8. 0.0021
9. 10.5
10. 25
11. 345.92
12. 88.59
13. 1/8
14. 1/10
15. 1/4
16. 2/5
17. 2-1/3
18. 56

Super-Sour Squares Special Order Form (p. 91)
Orange: 1.5 ÷ 3 = 0.5
Grape: 2.75 ÷ 25 = 0.11
Cherry: 0.5 ÷ 2 = 0.25
Blueberry: 10.25 ÷ 5 = 2.05
Lemon: 8.01 ÷ 6 = 1.335
Lime: 12.2 ÷ 5 = 2.44
Cherry: 3.9 ÷ 10 = 0.39
Grape: 31.5 ÷ 100 = 0.315

Practice Page #14 (p. 92)
1. 8.6
2. 6.5
3. 0.89
4. 26.8
5. 89.1
6. 3.124
7. 0.58
8. 0.24
9. 1.06
10. 4.45
Journal: Answers will vary.

Review Page #14 (p. 93)
1. 3.2
2. 3.2
3. 0.2
4. 125.9
5. 0.405
6. 2.02
7. 6.35
8. 2.02
9. 0.004
10. 1.5
11. 0.0048
12. 98.28
13. 4.18
14. 1.01
15. 5.15
16. 5/12
17. 1-11/35
18. 12
19. 2-1/4
20. 20